SELF-FULFILLMENT
Through ZIONISM

A STUDY IN JEWISH ADJUSTMENT

SELF-FULFILLMENT Through ZIONISM

A STUDY IN JEWISH ADJUSTMENT

Edited by SHLOMO BARDIN

Biography Index Reprint Series

BOOKS FOR LIBRARIES PRESS
FREEPORT, NEW YORK

Copyright © 1943 by
The American Zionist Youth Commission

Reprinted 1971 by arrangement with
The American Zionist Youth Foundation, Inc.

INTERNATIONAL STANDARD BOOK NUMBER:
0-8369-8076-X

LIBRARY OF CONGRESS CATALOG CARD NUMBER:
70-142605

PRINTED IN THE UNITED STATES OF AMERICA

CONTENTS

INTRODUCTION 5

I. THE PROBLEM

    L. B. NAMIER—*The Jews* 11

II. THE ANALYSIS

    KURT LEWIN—*Self-Hatred Among Jews* 25

III. THE SOURCES

    LOUIS ADAMIC—*The Man in a Quandary* 45

    RUTH JONAS BARDIN—*Marian Sanders' Story* 66

    JESSE SAMPTER—*A Confession* 77

    DR. HISSIN—*From a Diary* 83

    LOUIS E. LEVINTHAL—*Louis D. Brandeis* 86

    ALEXANDER BEIN—*Theodore Herzl* 103

IV. THE CONCLUSION 125

(The Guide material follows each article and biography)

INTRODUCTION

DID it ever occur to you that you yourself can, to a large extent, determine whether you are to be a happy, well-adjusted person, or not? So much of life is beyond your control, but in at least this one respect, there is an element of conscious choice. This crucial aspect of your life is your relationship to the Jewish people, and a decision on this question can influence every facet of your life.

For no Jew can feel entirely secure until he has come to some conclusion about what being a Jew means to him, unless he is perfectly clear in his own mind about the fate he desires for his people and to what degree he accepts their future as bound up with his own. *No* decision is a *negative* decision, and even worse, it means you relinquish the right to steer your own course in life.

Sometimes we feel that we want to be simply and unequivocally Americans without having to worry about the necessity to recognize ourselves as Jews. But you *are* a Jew and you *do* have an inescapable necessity to reckon with that fact in your life, too. Will you clearly, positively and proudly accept your Jewish people and its glorious past and its equally creative future in Eretz Yisrael, and in the rest of the world, or are you willing to continue unclear, uncertain and unhappy about the fact that you are born a Jew.

This study unit is designed to help you make the important decision about what your relationship to the Jewish people will be. Because it is easier to see a human problem and to think about the solutions to it, if you can vicariously experience what others have experienced, and what others have found satisfying or distressing solutions, we have collected here the biographies of Jews, case studies in Jewish adjustment. One of these Jews continues to reject all the implications of his Jewish birth; the others at first rejected (or were indifferent to) but later joyously accepted their people and their heritage.

To aid in setting the problem on a larger base, there is the introductory essay of L. B. Namier, a survey of our status today. We have thought it well too, to enlist the aid of an eminent social psychologist, Kurt Lewin, who has given much thought to the problem of minority groups and social relations. His study and analysis of Jewish self-hatred sheds a brilliant light on some of our unsuspected reactions and helps us to understand ourselves in relation to the rest of the world and thus to know how to choose more wisely for ourselves.

A careful study of Namier and Lewin and their applications in the biographies of Jews who have and who have not found a full and happy solution to their anomalous position in the world today, should aid you to escape the unhappy state of indecision. It should point the way to a clear, conscious choice of your Jewish position and make it possible for you to achieve self-fulfillment as a Jew and as an American.

TO THE GROUP LEADER

1. Read and discuss the introduction at the first meeting.
2. Assign the reading of Namier's "The Jews" to the group as a whole for careful discussion at the second meeting. Guide material is included in this study unit.
3. Have at least two people read and carefully prepare a report on Lewin's essay, "Self-Hatred." Use the guide and guide questions as the base for study. Every member of the group should read this paper.
4. At the beginning of the course assign one biography to each person for special preparation. All the group members should be reading all the biographies. Guide questions are included for the discussion of each biography. Call the attention of the group to the fact that after the guide questions to each biography, we have appended one or more references to further readings on the person, background or issues involved. Where pamphlets are referred to, they can be obtained on request at the office of the American Zionist Youth Commission, 381 Fourth Avenue, New York City. We urge you to make use of this collateral material.

   It would be best to begin the biographies with Dr. Steinberger. Then proceed in this order: Sanders, Sampter and Hissin, Brandeis and Herzl.

   Constant reference should be made to the Lewin material and the personality under discussion should be studied in terms of Lewin's point of view.
5. Urge members to be searching in their own experience for examples of people who have or who have not found themselves as Jews. It might be advisable too to study a case of some strong anti-Zionist whom a member of the group may know. Encourage them to contribute reports of such instances to the group at a meeting assigned for this purpose.

   In the analysis of personal biographies use the following outline as a guide:

   (a) Factors in family background leading to (a) security in the sense of Jewish belonging (b) security in terms of Jewish habits, values and knowledge.

   (b) When and how they met Zionism.

   (c) Its effect on the personality in terms of: imperviousness to anti-semitism, poise and clarity of aim in life.

   (d) Can you recognize the fading of symptoms of self-hatred and the emergence of a feeling of self-fulfillment when Zionism is completely accepted or, on the contrary, a continuing tension and restlessness where no decision is made or where the person consciously ignores his connection with his people?
6. Tie up the whole in a final session, guided by the concluding material.

THE PROBLEM

THE JEWS

By

L. B. NAMIER
Professor of Modern History in the University of Manchester (England)

WHO is a Jew? For large numbers of Gentiles, anyone whom they want to belittle or stigmatize. This type of Gentile, conscious of the slur which he puts upon our name, has in the past devised for us compassionate euphemisms, especially numerous in continental languages: "Israelites," "Hebrews," "Old Testamentarians," etc. Now the Nazis have invented "honorary Aryans" and, if it suits them, they allow a half-Jew with a Jewish father to establish his fitness for an honourable career by "proving" that, before he was born in wedlock (maybe half a century ago), his mother had committed adultery with an "Aryan." Lueger, the Jew-baiting Bürgermeister of Vienna, and Field-Marshal Goering are both credited with the saying: "It is for me to determine who is a Jew."

Whom are we Jews to consider a Jew? A prominent Zionist once remarked that, seeing how hard is the lot of the Jew, he accepts as such, without further question, anybody who claims to be one. On the Day of Atonement, before the most solemn prayer, the *Kol Nidre,* is said for those who have forsworn themselves, The Elders of the synagogue step forward and announce that these may re-enter and pray. At the hour of Israel's reunion with his God, there can be no enquiry into the past, no reproach, and no exclusion. And now in our history has come the Day of Atonement and the hour of the *Kol Nidre.* Those who were weak, or vain, or cowardly, or merely oblivious, who sought to evade sharing our common burden, and tried to forget and make others forget that they were Jews, or at least attempted to compromise with their Judaism and not be compromised by it, must be allowed to seek mental peace and moral comfort in a return to their God and to their nation. No other peace and comfort is the portion of any of us in the Dispersion.

In most countries some Jews have been allowed, at one period of history or another, under this or that garb, to rise to the highest offices and honours, to attain rank and power: as individuals, not as Jews. Yet there has hardly been one among them who at some stage in his career did not feel, closing on him and enveloping him, the miasmatic, choking film of that mysterious, undefinable "Jewish problem", so unlike anything his neighbours have to encounter; and who then did not wish it were given to him to live the life of a humble but normal human being, about whom no one "wonders" and has doubts, and who is not asked unanswerable questions. And the Jew is lucky if these are merely "questions" and not charges, imputations, invectives—the efflux of the non-Jew's neurotic imagination or wrought-up temper. The more the Jew explains, the greater the anger and suspicions of the non-Jew: for the one does not know what to ask, nor the other what to answer. It is the "Third Degree" drawn out through the ages, insidious and yet devoid of conscious purpose.

In the country where the Jews are given the fairest deal, in Great Britain (and the same applied to some extent to France before her defeat), they have a chance, but not always an equal chance, of doing work; and for whatever good work they accomplish they receive credit. But if a Jew errs, or merely incurs unpopularity, a resentment rises against him far more violent and venomous than were he a non-Jew. Edwin Montagu's Indian policy having displeased many Conservatives, his dismissal brought on in the House of Commons a scene of savage delight betokening a virulent anger such as has never been kindled by the numerous non-Jews who have bungled along the same path. Nor would in France the hatred even against a Socialist Prime Minister have risen to such fatal heights had not Blum been a Jew—the slogan of the Right Wing defeatists, "rather Hitler than Blum", expressed more than mere loathing of Socialism. And what ineffable bitterness there is in the remark said to have been made in the hour of defeat by Mandel, the Minister who never wavered, that he could save France if only his name were Dupont! It seems doubtful whether "Rima," or any other work of Epstein, would have evoked such strident, and sometimes even defacing, dissent had his name been Evans. Many of us are happy to acknowledge the eminently fair treatment which we and our work have received in this country. Still, in every one of us there is, deep down, the consciousness that we cannot afford to slip; a fall for us is harder and more irretrievable than for a non-Jew.

Not even in this country does the Jew enjoy the same moral freedom to express his view, especially in politics, as the non-Jew. If a Socialist, he is suspect of Bolshevism; if a Conservative, he is a "bloated capitalist." Certainly not every non-Jew feels that way, and of those who do, few will show it: for Englishmen hate being unfair or rude. But there is seldom a cloudless sky over the Jew—as he speaks, shadows pass across, and feelings are aroused which, though rarely fixed in words, are present and real. Occasionally they find vent in an invitation to the Jew "to go back to his own country"—as if he had in the Diaspora a country which was his own and which would welcome him. When Sir Alfred Mond once advocated in the Commons Empire migration, which in any non-Jew would have been an irreproachable subject, a member of the extreme Left hurled at him the reply that it was not for a German Jew to tell Scotsmen to leave their country. When, some time in 1937, I defended the Treaty of Versailles in the presence of a certain Left Wing intellectual, he very nearly screamed at me that after all the years which I had lived in this country I was a complete foreigner, for every Englishman knew that it was a "bad treaty;" and when I said that we ought to have checked Hitler at an earlier stage by a preventive war, he replied: "I am a 100 percent Aryan—what would you say if I justified Hitler's conduct as making preventive war against the Jews?" This man is not an anti-Semite; he has helped Jewish refugees; he is, in fact, a League of Nations internationalist; but feeling irritated at a Jew who happens to be a Conservative, he talked as a Fascist would to a Jew of the Left.

No doubt the fact that many of us are newcomers or the children of immigrants, have foreign names and foreign accents, adds to the difficulties, dislikes, and friction; but the "native-born" Jews of so-called "old lineage" grossly deceive themselves if they think that were it not for those "strangers" they would be looked upon as indistinguishable from other Englishmen. Every Jew must have come here at one time or another; and even in America the Jews are the only ones who cannot claim to have come over on the *Mayflower*—we miss every boat, and all the waters are to us "rivers of Babylon." We shift about in the Diaspora, driven by grievous disappointments, if not by downright persecutions and by bitter need; and our movements add to to the discomfort of those who moved before us. The game of musical chairs goes on, the pace quickens till it becomes a breathless, giddy gyration, a dizzy round, a maelstrom. Polish Jews in Russia, Russian Jews in Poland, Polish Jews in Germany, German Jews in England, every kind of Jew in America—this merry-go-round of would-be-redeeming migrations changes in time into a wheel on which we are broken. For in the Exile the Jews are truly at rest only there where "the prisoners are at ease together" and "hear not the voice of the oppressor."

A man, to attain full moral stature and intellectual poise, to enjoy life and be socially creative, has to be at ease: this is seldom given to Jews who try to overcome the Galuth (Exile) by both accepting and denying it. While suffering slurs, often hard to define but always implying inferiority, they try to make themselves and others believe that relations are satisfactory, indeed normal. Such a Jew will tell you that he for one has never experienced any "discrimination," that he is treated by the Gentiles exactly as if he was one of them; he seems to take pride in it, and receives as a boon what normal people assume to be their birthright. A Scotsman with whom I had only a very superficial acquaintance, on my telling him that I was a Jew, said: "I do not know how you will like what I am going to say, but you are the first Jew I ever liked." I replied: "Would it interest you to know whether I like Scotsmen?" He admitted that it would not. "Then why do you expect me to be interested in what you feel about Jews?" He saw the point, as will any sane non-Jew to whom it is put. But when making his remark—not in the best taste—he probably expected me to be both flattered and hurt, to make excuses for the Jews which would be self-accusations and set him in judgment over us. To most people it is pleasing to establish their superiority and then to be censorious, indulgent, open-minded, and unconvinced. This is the game to which Jews submit when they worry too much about what non-Jews think of us: it is difficult to endure it with dignity, and to pass through it unscathed. The Jews have suffered the most incredible persecutions and tortures in the two thousand years of Dispersion. But so long as they remain a coherent, self-contained community, with a consciousness and a national pride of their own, they preserve their strength and vitality: and contempt or insults from their neighbours do not affect them any more than, say, those of eighteenth-century Chinese would have affected Englishmen resident among them. It was the semi-toleration accepted by the assimilated Jews which turned so many of them into neurotics.

Every man carries in him and with him a communal memory and inheritance, the more distinctive the longer the conscious life of his race. Ours is the longest continuous history, most varied on the surface, least varied at its core, unique in character. On the rock of our existence, the Book, other nations have built, while we in the Dispersion have had to enter their abodes, adopting their languages, undergoing their influence, fitting ourselves into their modes of living, working within frameworks set to us by them; dissolving all the time, and yet surviving. Because of that "remnant," people ask why the Jews do not melt? Every glacier melts in parts, at given seasons; and some have disappeared altogether; but to a certain type of intelligence, the glacier which is not, and the glacier which is, equally demonstrate the fact that glaciers do not melt. In the present world there is not enough warmth to melt down all the glaciers, nor to absorb even those Jews who would wish to be absorbed. For such there must be, at all times and in all countries: in the circumstances of the Dispersion, assimilation is a natural process, and those who succumb to it are neither the worst, nor necessarily the weakest; we all undergo assimilation in some measure or other; but those who long to be joined to their neighbours closer than they are, are the most unhappy among the Jews. For the desire to be "assimilated" is a confession of inferiority, an attempt to divest oneself of one's own inheritance in order to share in that of others. He who does that submits, without the will or means to stand up for himself, to the scrutiny and judgment of people for whom he feels attachment and an often uncritical admiration, but who do not necessarily feel any for him.

What a life, to be continually on trial and under examination! Uncertainty breeds anxiety, and anxiety provokes critical attention. Cold eyes glance furtively at the unwanted Jew; his presence produces subdued alertness; even if there is no open hostility, there is a more than ordinary readiness to find fault; the less people are willing to admit prejudice, the more eager they subconsciously are to justify it(and prejudice is the universal attitude of men towards strangers not strong enough to command their respect and approval). Speak out, and there is nothing more to be said; suppress things, and you cause discomfort and irritation. Most of the peculiarities with which the Jew is taunted (and sometimes tainted) are the result of deeper *malaise*. Harried, he is blamed for being restless; kept out or kept down, he is described as pushing and assertive; hurt, he searches for compensations and is called vain, blatant, or self-indulgent; insecure, he yearns for standing, power, and wealth; which sometimes protect him, but more often expose him the more to attack. Even in the most ordinary intercourse, uncertainty is apt to react unfavourably on his bearing. He is too eager to please, too affable, perhaps too intimate; too intent and emphatic; he shows off and talks too much—in short, he is self-conscious and embarrassed, and his company becomes exhausting. In public life he is too patriotic and public-spirited (for he continually pays entrance fees and ransom); or, having experienced social injustice, he becomes the spokesman of the injured and aggrieved—a part we have often played, and for which we have almost invariably paid the penalty.

At present the Jew is, if not a "refugee," at least a perpetual evacuee from a non-existing home. Great numbers of Britons have in this war learnt how it tastes to be an evacuee; yet much greater numbers learnt how evacuees, even of one's own race, appear to half-willing hosts—"them evacuees (a nasty, crafty-looking lot)," says Nathaniel Gubbins in the *Sunday Express*, speaking with the unmistakable voice of Every-man. And there is a phantasy of his which comes to my mind as I write about the Jew "on trial and under examination."

> The Dog and The Cat had grown so big and The Man and The Woman had shrunk so small that it was The Dog who was taking The Man to the local Man Show . . .

Dog and Cat were discussing the peculiarities of the human breed, while The Cat was grooming The Man for the Show.

>The Man, bored and irritated, escaped The Cat for a moment and ran to The Dog . . .
>"Come here, sir", said The Cat.
>"Never mind, Mansy Boy", said The Dog, patting The Man's head. "It'll soon be over."

If only the Jews could for once grow so big, be so firmly rooted in the soil, feel so perfectly at ease, and the non-Jews find themselves, by some miracle, circumstanced as the Jews are at present! The decent Jews would then befriend them, and occasionally lecture them in a kindly manner; and the nasty ones would indulge in spiteful criticism; and together they would, having become "Gentile-conscious," analyze "Gentile peculiarities" and discuss "The Gentile problem." I wish Nathaniel Gubbins would develop this theme; it would make people laugh, and some might stop and consider.

While emotionally the would-be assimilated suffer most, we are all in some degree assimilated to our neighbours, and dependent on them. As between individuals, I could ask the Scotsman why he expected me to be interested in what he felt about the Jews when he was not interested in what I felt about the Scots; but in the mass, so long as we retain any interest in life, we must care about those who can render it tolerable for us or intolerable. I eschew speaking here of countries where the flood of anti-Semitism has broken all dams, where insulting the Jew is the law of the land, and killing him no longer murder, where the Jews are robbed of their possessions, debarred from earning a living, and finally herded together in overcrowded ghettos to await a slow, lingering death from starvation, exhaustion, and disease. I eschew speaking even of milder forms of anti-Semitic action, such as prevailed in pre-war Poland or Rumania. I speak of countries where the Jews experience nothing worse than discreet relegation or special adverteny, and suffer of *malaise* and not of persecutions; where the Jews congratulate themselves on their luck, and the non-Jews on their generosity; but where, none the less, anti-Semitism is like a dark cloud on the horizon, and friends come to the Jew with worried faces to tell him how much they are disturbed by the rapid growth of anti-Semitism which they have noticed recently. And this is usually said with a faint suggestion that the Jew can, and should, do something about it; although he can do about as much to deal with the rising storm, if it does rise, as men in a foundering barque can to assuage a raging sea. Had France in 1918 suffered defeat, and not Germany, new Déroulèdes and Drumonts would have arisen, and not Hitler.

Every nation keeps its own ledger; ours alone is kept by strangers, who place the achievements of individual Jews to their own credit, and leave us only with the debit side. And there is a vague belief in the Gentile mind that all Jews are marvellously knit together; therefore in some way responsible for every single one among them. If Smith operates in the "black market," Smith does it; If Cohen, it is the Jew. Whenever some specially unpleasant or provoking incident occurs, Jews who by no stretch of imagination could be connected with it, murmur: "I hope to God the fellow is not a Jew." When Hitler imposed a fantastic fine on an already ruined German Jewry because one young Jew, driven mad by the sufferings inflicted on his parents, had killed a German diplomat, he merely condensed and exhibited in hideous, grotesque exaggeration (as he so often does) an idea deeply ingrained and widely diffused among the Gentiles. Without the least power to control individual members of our race, who frequently have lost all touch with us, we are expected to achieve in discipline what a totalitarian dictatorship could hardly undertake. On the other hand, the merit and achievements of individual Jews are not as a rule reflected in the Gentile attitude to Jewry. When a non-Jew states, "I have many friends among the Jews," the Jew knows that this is not a preface to compliments: that a "but" will inevitably follow, leading up to anti-Semitic, or at least to highly critical remarks.

A book could be written on the bitter absurdities of the treatment accorded to the Jews: another, proving that they themselves are largely responsible for the treatment they receive; and a third, to show that, seeing the conditions under which the Jews are made to live, they have preserved a remarkable and very creditable measure of sanity and decency. But the obvious conclusion of it all is that a situation which produces such results should not be continued indefinitely. Anti-Semitism did not start with Hitler, nor will it end with him: but it has been a trump card in his hand, as in the hands of innumerable smaller demagogues and scoundrels. In the interest both of the Jews and the non-Jews the ground must be cleared at last. But this will not be done by "seven maids with seven mops," were they to sweep for a century.

The "emancipation" movement of the "assimilationist" arose in the individualist era; it knows only Jews, but no Jewish nation. Its leaders, rich and educated, had entered Gentile society, and approached the problem of their own people internally in terms of "philanthropy," externally in terms of "toleration." They planned to re-shape the lives of millions while treating them as so many individuals—an impossible task. At the same time, they wished to preserve the existence of Jewish communities: there was a duality of purpose resulting in an unstable compromise. They believed, and wished others to believe ,that a national religious tradition and separate racial identity need not interfere with absorption by other nations. More logical were those who attempted amalgamation; but even this, as a mass movement, merely produces Marranos or "non-Aryan Christians." Those who treat the Jewish problem as the sum-total of innumerable individual problems, render it insoluble; for each individual case is troublesome, and their aggregate unbearable. Moreover, the other nations do not cease to sense the Jews as a people apart, and express it in their exaggerated belief in Jewish "oneness;" but the Jews, who, by reducing themselves to the level of a nondescript, a-historic group, cast away the dignity of a nation, court and incur indignities. For a sense of grandeur men derive only from the conscious collectivity—the nation. The greatness of a nation raises the status of its members; but the merit and achievements of individual Jews now lack the framework which would give them their full value. The first step towards a solution of the Jewish problem is for us to recover our historic national consciousness; then and then only, can we expect the non-Jews to count with us. A nation is not a mere sum-total of the individuals who compose it; it transcends them all, and possesses weight and values which none of them can claim individually.

Every creature leaves its trail on the face of the globe, and every star affects the orbits of the other stars. Not one nation, however insignificant, can without distortion be omitted from the world's history: but remove the Jews and history becomes incomprehensible. We enter into everything that has happened in the last two thousand years, in which history was made by the interplay between creeds of Hebraic origin and the nations affected by them. Whether "the tables were the work of God, and the writing was the writing of God," or whether they were the work of the People; whether the Sermon on the Mount was spoken by the Son of God, or by a son of the People; these events occurred in our midst, are part of our history, have determined our fate, and through us the fate of the world. Nineteen centuries ago our people divided: one branch, the Hebrew Nazarenes, carried into the world our national faith coupled with their new tidings, the other, as a closed community, preserved the old tradition. Yet both were part of one nation, and both are part of our national history. Only by seeing them as one whole shall we recover the full sense and greatness of our history. Those who went into the ways of the Gentiles, have permeated and transformed the heritage of other nations, and transmitted to them a creed which guides and binds, is cherished or endured. The others became the "remnant" which awaits the Return "that they may live." The relation of men to every creed has been mixed in character; the highest intensity produces a polarity of feelings—love tinged with hatred. How much of the hatred which turned against the Jewish remnant was hostility to Christianity, diverted against those among whom it had originated? At last in our time, enemies have arisen to the Jews, the worst we ever had, conscious of that connexion. The Nazis started with an onslaught against the Jews, and part of Hitler's success was due to the widespread—often only half-avowed, half-conscious—sympathy which there was for that onslaught among all the nations. Sincere Christians never felt it, and were among the first to see the true face of Nazism; which by now is openly turned against Christianity and all its values.

Hitler will be defeated: and yet, unless the Jewish problem is faced in the light of history and with a courageous, realistic approach, it will continue to poison our lives and the minds of non-Jews. Normality must be our aim: to be no longer either "prodigies" or outcasts, or both. Jews with a national consciousness and purpose must be given an honest chance to build on the foundations which they have laid in Palestine: a Jewish National State must arise there once more(and then, after we have ceased to be a "peculiar people," even the position of those who remain in Dispersion will become more normal). There must be a country where Jews can live, work, and amuse themselves as they please; be good, bad, great, or ridiculous; but, like all nations, among themselves, not under the eyes of strangers. What otherwise the outcome of the Return will be, is beside the point. Some Zionists occasionally engage in high-minded, highfalutin discourses about the "magnificent contribution which we shall then be enabled to make to the common stock of humanity"— and demonstrate therein once more the Galuth mentality of men who feel beholden to pay tribute, for which they seek compensation in high-brow superiorities. If, having concluded the Great Journey, we shall become altogether humdrum and mediocre, that, too, will be our own affair: but our children will have a better life—and this suffices. No nation need justify itself in its own home, and it matters little what nations think of each other. "The political body has no heart . . ." wrote an anonymous Irish pamphleteer in 1779, "and nations have affections for themselves, though they have none for each other. . . . There is no such thing as political humanity." Scattered groups without a centre must not be exposed to the impact of nations. National emancipation is the meaning and essence of Zionism.

Reprinted from:
"CONFLICTS" By Permission of McMillan & Co.

GUIDE TO NAMIER'S "THE JEWS"

We are asking you to read this article first, because it seems best to state the problem presented in the study unit. As you read it carefully, notice these important points:

1. Who is a Jew? In your opinion, who is a Jew? Can you define him? Notice Namier's simple, common-sense conclusion.

2. Even when a Jew achieves a successful career, the spectre of the "Jewish problem" never leaves him entirely, and if he fails or sins, greater fury pursues him *because* he is a Jew.
   Notice too, how the successful Jew is seldom recognized as a Jew but how surely the Jews as a whole are always included in the sins or faults of any Jew.

3. What is the implication of Namier's position that we are everywhere comparatively newcomers, recent immigrants, forced again and again to move and therefore always "refugees"?

4. Notice Namier's point (p. 14) that to attain the best development of the personality, requires ease, freedom from tension.

5. What are the conditions necessary for establishing ease in any environment, according to Namier? (p. 15).
   (a) "A coherent, self-contained community."
   (b) A national pride of our own.

6. The Jewish problem is insoluble if it is treated as "the sum total of innumerable individual problems" (p. 19). This unhappy tension between us and our neighbors has persisted for many generations. No individual solution can succeed because it does not take account of the fact that we are not 16 million scattered digits, but a unit, a number, a group recognized and feared and hated as a group.

7. What are the steps toward a solution of the Jewish problem according to Namier?
   Step I. To achieve or "recover our historic national consciousness", i.e., to recognize the reality and creativity of Israel.
   Step II. A return to normal status, not always "visitors" or "foreigners", but a normal people in its own land.
   Step III. The result of Step I, plus Step II, is to normalize the status of every individual Jew, no matter where he lives.

8. Identification with the cause of Zionism releases the tension, and brings self-fulfillment. How?
   (a) By accepting your status as a Jew, by recognizing the value of the Hebrew language, culture and tradition;
   (b) by helping to establish our people in its own land;
   (c) by identifying yourself with the pioneer spirit in Eretz Yisrael.

THE ANALYSIS

SELF-HATRED AMONG JEWS
By
Kurt Lewin

THAT self-hatred is present among Jews is a fact that the non-Jew would hardly believe, but which is well known among the Jews themselves. It is a phenomenon which has been observed ever since the emancipation of the Jews. Professor Lessing treated this topic in Germany (1930) in a book, *Der Jüdische Selbsthass* ("Jewish Self-Hate"). Novels like that of Ludwig Lewisohn (*Island Within*, 1928), which pictures the New York Jew around 1930, and that of Schnitzler, who deals with the problems of the Austrian Jew in the period around 1900, are striking in the similarity of the problems which they show to exist. In these different countries, the same conflicts arise and Jews of the various social strata and professions attempt the same variety of solutions.

Jewish self-hatred is both a group phenomenon and an individual phenomenon. In Europe, outstanding examples of a hostile sentiment in one Jewish group against another were those of the German or Austrian Jew against the East European Jew, and, more recently, the attitude of the French Jew toward the German Jew. That all the troubles the Jews had in Germany were due to the bad conduct of the East European Jew was an opinion not infrequently heard among German Jews. In this country, the resentment of the Spanish Jew against the immigrating German Jew, and the hostility of the latter to the East European Jew form a parallel to the European situation.

Speaking in terms of individuals rather than groups, the self-hatred of a Jew may be directed against the Jews as a group, against a particular fraction of the Jews, against his own family, or against himself. It may be directed against Jewish institutions, Jewish mannerisms, Jewish language, or Jewish ideals.

There is an almost endless variety of forms which Jewish self-hatred may take. Most of them, and the most dangerous forms, are a kind of indirect, under-cover self-hatred. If I should count the instances where I have encountered open and straightforward contempt among Jews, I could name but a few. The most striking, for me, was the behavior of a well-educated Jewish refugee from Austria on the occasion of his meeting a couple of other Jewish refugees. In a tone of violent hatred, he burst out into a defense of Hitler on the ground of the undesirable characteristics of the German Jew.

But these are rare incidents. In most cases, expression of hatred of the Jew against his fellow Jew or against himself as a Jew is more subtle. This hatred is so blended with other motives that it is difficult to decide in any one particular case whether or not self-hatred is involved. Take the well-educated Jewish atheist who finally consented to deliver an address at a temple. During the service which preceded his talk, he told me about the pain he experiences on seeing a *talith* (prayer shawl), and how this aversion was first implanted in him by his father's negative attitude toward the synagogue. Have we to deal here with a form of anti-Jewish sentiment or just the great aversion of the atheist for religion? Does the rich Jewish merchant who refuses to contribute anything to a Jewish charity hate his own people or is he just miserly? The Jewish head of a department or a store may seem to lean over backward in regard to employing Jews; but perhaps what he does is actually the maximum than can be done under the circumstances.

It occurs infrequently—although it does happen once in a while—that a Jewish person frankly admits that he hates to be together with Jews. Most of the people who avoid Jewish associations have "good reasons." They are so busy with non-Jewish associations that they "simply don't have time." The boy who prefers "Ethical Culture" or "Christian Science" to Judaism will tell you that he is not running away from things Jewish, but is attracted by the values of the other groups.

In some cases, of course, these "reasons" may actually be the real reasons. Still, there are certain facts which make one wonder. The non-Jewish partner in a mixed marriage will frequently be much more realistic in regard to the education of his children.

He seems to see the necessity for the child's growing up with a clear understanding of his being either inside or outside the Jewish group. The Jewish partner often takes the position that children in the United States can grow up simply as human beings. He would deny that he is guided by the same sentiment which has prompted many rich Austrian and German Jews to baptize their children and otherwise to link them as much as possible with typically non-Jewish groups.

However, if the aversion of our atheist for the symbols of Jewish religion were his only motive, he should feel the same aversion against symbols of any organized religion. That that is not the case shows that something else underlies his behavior. The Jewish child from an unorthodox home who tells his mother, "If I see the old Jewish man praying with his *talith*, it makes me feel good; it is as if I pray myself", shows that religious indifference does not necessarily lead to such an aversion. Why does the merchant who refuses to contribute to the Jewish cause spend lavishly on every non-Jewish activity? Why do camps which accommodate only Jewish children hire only non-Jewish counselors and have a Christian Sunday service, but no Jewish songs or other Jewish activities?

SELF-HATRED AS A SOCIAL PHENOMENON

An attempt has been made to explain Jewish self-hatred as the outgrowth of certain deep-seated human instincts. This behavior seems to be a prime example of what Freud calls the drive to self-destruction or the "death instinct." However, an explanation like that is of little value. Why does the Englishman not have the same amount of hatred against his countrymen, or the German against the German, as the Jew against the Jew? If the self-hatred were the result of a general instinct, we should expect its degree to depend only on the personality of the individual. But the amount of self-hatred the individual Jew shows seems to depend far more on his attitude toward Judaism than on his personality.

Jewish self-hatred is a phenomenon which has its parallel in many underprivileged groups. One of the better known and most extreme cases of self-hatred can be found among American Negroes. Negroes distinguish within their group four or five strata according to skin shade—the lighter the skin the higher the strata.

This discrimination among themselves goes so far that a girl with a light skin may refuse to marry a man with a darker skin. A sentiment of self-hatred which is less strong but still clearly distinguishable may also be found among the second generation of Greek, Italian, Polish and other immigrants to this country.

The dynamics of self-hatred and its relation to social facts become apparent by a somewhat closer examination. A Jewish girl at a fashionable midwestern university confided she had told her friends that her parents were American-born, although actually her father is a first-generation immigrant from the East, speaking with a strong accent. Now she has a bad conscience toward her father, whom she actually loves, and plans to leave the university. Why did she do it? She felt that if her parentage were known, she would not be eligible to certain more fashionable circles on the campus.

The cause of this action against the family group is rather obvious: the individual has certain expectations and goals for the future. Belonging to his group is seen as an impediment to reaching those goals. This leads to a tendency to set himself apart from the group. In the case of the student, this resulted in a conflict with the psychological tie to the family, a conflict which she was unable to stand. However, it is easy to see how such a frustration may lead to a feeling of hatred against one's own group as the source of the frustration.

A Jewish lady, dining in a fashionable restaurant with a non-Jewish friend, was greatly annoyed by a couple of other guests who behaved in a loud manner and were obviously somewhat intoxicated. For one reason or another, she had the feeling that these people might be Jewish. Her friend made a remark which clearly indicated that they were not Jewish. The lady felt greatly relieved, and from that moment on was amused rather than annoyed by their boisterousness. Such incidents are of daily occurrence. The outstanding phenomenon here seems to be an extreme sensitivity in the Jewish woman regarding the behavior of other Jews, similar to the sensitivity of a mother about the behavior of her children when they perform in public. Common to this case and to that of the student is the feeling of the individual that his position is threatened or that his future is endangered through his being identified with a certain group.

The sensitivity in regard to the conduct of other members of a group is but an expression of a fundamental fact of group life, namely, interdependence of fate. It is revealing that Jews who claim to be free of Jewish ties still frequently show a great sensitivity. It indicates that, in spite of their words, these people are somehow aware of the social reality. Indeed, life, freedom, and the pursuit of happiness of every Jewish community in America and every individual American Jew depends in a specific way on the social status which the Jews as a group have in the more inclusive community of the United States. In case Hitler should win the war, this special interdependence of fate will become the most important determining factor in the life of every single Jew. If Hitler should lose, this interdependence will still be one of the dominant factors for the lives of our children.

THE FORCES TOWARD AND AWAY FROM GROUP MEMBERSHIP

Analytically, one can distinguish two types of forces in regard to the member of any group, one type drawing him into the group and keeping him inside, the other driving him away from the group. The sources of the forces toward the group may be manifold: perhaps the individual feels attracted to other members of the group, perhaps the other members draw him in, maybe he is interested in the goal of the group or feels in accord with its ideology, or he may prefer this group to being alone. Similarly, the forces away from the group may be the result of any sort of disagreeable features of the group itself, or they may be an expression of the greater attractiveness of an outside group.

If the balance between the forces toward and away from the group is negative, the individual will leave the group if no other factors intervene. Under "free" conditions, therefore, a group will contain only those members for whom the positive forces are stronger than the negative. If a group is not attractive enough to a sufficient number of individuals, it will disappear.

We must realize, however, that the forces toward and away from the group are not always an expression of the persons' own needs. They may be imposed upon the individual by some external power. In other words, an individual may be forced against his will to stay inside a group he would like to leave, or he may be kept outside a group he would like to join. For instance, a dictator closes the borders of the country so that nobody may leave. A fashionable circle keeps many people outside who would like to be included.

COHESIVE AND DISRUPTIVE FORCES IN AN UNDERPRIVILEGED GROUP

An important factor for the strength of the forces toward and away from the group is the degree to which the fulfillment of the individual's own needs is furthered or hampered by his membership in the group. Some groups, like the Chamber of Commerce or the labor union, exist for the express purpose of furthering the interests of their members. On the other hand, membership in any group limits freedom of action for the individual member to some degree. Being married and having a pleasant and efficient wife may be a great help for the husband in achieving his ambitions, but marriage can be a great handicap, too. By and large, one can say that the more the reaching of the individual's goal is furthered or hindered by the group, the more likely it is that the balance of forces toward or away from the group will be positive or negative.

This analysis permits a general statement in regard to members of socially privileged and underprivileged groups. To gain status is one of the outstanding factors determining the behavior of the individual in our society. The privileged group, in addition, usually offers its members more and hinders them less than does the less privileged group. For these reasons, the members of the élite in any country have a strong positive balance in the direction of staying in the élite group. Besides, if an individual wants to leave this élite, he is usually able to do so without hindrance (although there are exceptions).

The member of an underprivileged group is more hampered by his group belongingness. In addition, the tendency to gain status means a force away from such a group. At the same time, we find that in the case of any socially underprivileged group, free mobility across the boundary is limited or entirely prevented by a lack of ability or by external forces. The more privileged majority or an influential section of this majority prohibits free mobility. In every socially underprivileged group, therefore, there are a number of members for whom the balance of the forces toward and away from the group is such that they would prefer to leave it. They are kept inside the group not by their own needs, but by forces which are imposed upon them. This has a far-reaching effect on the atmosphere, structure and organization of every underprivileged group and on the psychology of its members.

GROUP LOYALTY AND NEGATIVE CHAUVINISM

In every group one can distinguish strata which are culturally more central, and others which are more peripheral. The central stratum contains those values, habits, ideas and traditions which are considered most essential and representative for the group. For the musician, this means the ideal musician; for the Englishman, what he considers to be typically English.

People who are loyal to a group have a tendency to rate the more central layers higher. In other words, the average Englishman is "proud" to be English and would dislike being called un-English. Frequently there is a tendency to over-rate the central layer. In such a case we speak of a "100% Americanism" or, more generally, of chauvinism. But a positive rating of the central layers is a logical result of group loyalty and a very essential factor in keeping a group together. Without such loyalty no group can progress and prosper.

Those individuals who would like to leave a group do not have this loyalty. In an underprivileged group, many of these individuals are, nevertheless, forced to stay within the group. As a result, we find in every underprivileged group a number of persons ashamed of their membership. In the case of the Jews, such a Jew will try to move away as far as possible from things Jewish. On his scale of values, he will place those habits, appearances or attitudes which he considers to be particularly Jewish *not* particularly high; he will rank them low. He will show a "negative chauvinism."

This situation is much aggravated by the following fact: A person for whom the balance is negative will move as far away from the center of Jewish life as the outside majority permits. He will stay on this barrier and be in a constant state of frustration. Actually, he will be more frustrated than those members of the minority who keep psychologically well inside the group.

We know from experimental psychology and psychopathology that such frustration leads to an all-around state of high tension with a generalized tendency to aggression. The aggression should, logically, be directed against the majority, which is what hinders the minority member from leaving his group. However, the majority has, in the eyes of these persons, higher status. And besides, the majority is much too powerful to be attacked. Experiments have shown that, under these conditions, aggression is likely to be turned against one's own group or against one's self.[1]

THE POWER OF THE ATTITUDES OF THE PRIVILEGED GROUP

The tendency toward aggression against one's own group, under these circumstances, is strengthened by an additional factor. Mark Twain tells the story of a Negro who was brought up as a white child. When he turns against his mother in a most vicious and cowardly way, his mother says, "That's the nigger in you." In other words, she has accepted the white man's verdict in characterizing some of the worst features as typical of the Negro.

It is recognized in sociology that the members of the lower social strata tend to accept the fashions, values and ideals of the higher strata. In the case of the underprivileged group it means that their opinions about themselves are greatly influenced by the low esteem the majority has for them. This infiltration of the views and values of what Maurice Pekarsky has called the "gatekeeper" necessarily heightens the tendency of the Jew with a negative balance to cut himself loose from things Jewish. The more typically Jewish people are, or the more typically Jewish a cultural symbol or behavior pattern is, the more distasteful they will appear to this person. Being unable to cut himself entirely loose from his Jewish connections and his Jewish past, the hatred turns upon himself.

ORGANIZATION OF UNDERPRIVILEGED GROUPS

Members of the majority are accustomed to think of a minority as a homogeneous group which they can characterize by a stereotype like "the Jew" or "the Negro." It has been shown that this

---

[1] K. Lewin, R. Lippitt, and R. K. White, "Patterns of aggressive behavior in experimentally created 'social climates,'" *Journal of Social Psychology*, 10, No. 2 (1939), 271-299.

stereotype is created in the growing child by the social atmosphere in which he grows up, and that the degree of prejudice is practically independent of the amount and kind of actual experience which the individual has had with members of the minority group.[2]

Actually, *every* group, including every economically or otherwise underprivileged group, contains a number of social strata. There exists, however, the following difference between the typical structure of a privileged and an underprivileged group. The forces acting on an individual member of a privileged group are directed toward the central layers of that group. The forces acting on a member of an underprivileged group are directed away from the central area, toward the periphery of the group and, if possible, toward the still higher status of the majority. The member would leave if the barrier set up by the majority did not prevent him. This picture represents the psychological situation of those members of the underprivileged group who have a basically negative balance. It is the structure of a group of people who are fundamentally turned against themselves.

It is clear that an effective organization of a group becomes more difficult the more it contains members having a negative balance, and the stronger this negative balance is. It is a well-known fact that the task of organizing a group which is economically or otherwise underprivileged is seriously hampered by those members whose real goal is to leave the group rather than to promote it. This deep-seated conflict of goals within an underprivileged group is not always clear to the members themselves. But it is one reason why even a large underprivileged group which would be able to obtain equal rights if it were united for action can be kept rather easily in an inferior position.

LEADERS FROM THE PERIPHERY

It is particularly damaging for the organization and action of a minority group that certain types of leaders are bound to arise in it. In any group, those sections are apt to gain leadership which are more generally successful. In a minority group, individual members who are economically successful, or who have distin-

---
[2] Eugene L. Horowitz, "The development of attitudes toward the Negro," *Arch. of Psychol.*, 1936, No. 194.

guished themselves in their professions, usually gain a higher degree of acceptance by the majority group. This places them culturally on the periphery of the underprivileged group and makes them more likely to be "marginal" persons. They frequently have a negative balance and are particularly eager to have their "good connections" not endangered by too close a contact with those sections of the underprivileged group which are not acceptable to the majority. Nevertheless, they are frequently called for leadership by the underprivileged group because of their status and power. They themselves are usually eager to accept the leading role in the minority, partly as a substitute for gaining status in the majority, partly because such leadership makes it possible for them to have and maintain additional contact with the majority.

As a result, we find the rather paradoxical phenomenon of what one might call "the leader from the periphery." Instead of having a group led by people who are proud of the group, who wish to stay in it and to promote it, we see minority leaders who are lukewarm toward the group, who may, under a thin cover of loyalty, be fundamentally eager to leave the group, or who try to use their power outright for acts of negative chauvinism. Having achieved a relatively satisfactory status among non-Jews, these individuals are chiefly concerned with maintaining the status quo and so try to soft-pedal any action which might arouse the attention of the non-Jew. These Jews would never think of accusing Knudsen of "double loyalty" for presiding at an American Danish rally, but they are so accustomed to viewing Jewish events with the eyes of the anti-Semite that they are afraid of the accusation of double loyalty in the case of any outspoken Jewish action. If there is "danger" of a Jew's being appointed to the Supreme Court, they will not hesitate to warn the President against such an action.

As stated in the beginning, it may be difficult to determine in a given case exactly where the boundary between Jewish chauvinism, normal loyalty, and negative chauvinism may lie. However, our analysis should make it clear that an unmanly and unwise (because unrealistic) hush-hush policy springs from the same forces of negative chauvinism or fear as Jewish self-hatred does. In fact, it is one of the most damaging varieties of Jewish self-hatred.

There are indications that the percentage of such people among leading members of the American Jewish community has increased since the first World War. In spite of the disastrous consequences which this policy had for the Jews of Germany, there are probably more Jews in America today who have a negative balance than there were in 1910.

On the other hand, the development of Palestine, the recent history of the European Jews, and the threat of Hitlerism have made the issues more clear. A few Jews, such as the infamous Captain Naumann in Germany, have become fascistic themselves under the threat of fascism. However, many Jews who had lost close contact with Judaism have come back under the threat of nazism in Europe. The history of revolutions teaches us that the most active and efficient leadership of the underprivileged has come from certain individuals who left the privileged groups and voluntarily linked their fate with that of the minority. These people must have had, for one reason or another, a particularly strong positive balance of the forces toward and away from the group. It would be in agreement with historical experience if there were found to be efficient leaders among those who have re-entered the ranks of the conscious Jew.

WHAT CAN BE DONE ABOUT JEWISH SELF-HATRED?

Self-hatred seems to be a psychopathological phenomenon, and its prevention may seem mainly a task for the psychiatrist. However, modern psychology knows that many psychological phenomena are but an expression of a social situation in which the individual finds himself. In a few cases, Jewish self-hatred may grow out of a neurotic or otherwise abnormal personality, but in the great majority of cases it is a phenomenon in persons of normal mental health. In other words, it is a social-psychological phenomenon, even though it usually influences deeply the total personality. In fact, neurotic trends in Jews are frequently the result of their lack of adjustment to just such group problems.

Jewish self-hatred will die out only when actual equality of status with the non-Jew is achieved. Only then will the enmity against one's own group decrease to the relatively insignificant proportions characteristic of the majority group's. Sound self-criticism will replace it. This does not mean that nothing can be done meanwhile. After all, we do have a great many Jews who can hardly be classified as anti-Semitic.

The only way to avoid Jewish self-hatred in its various forms is a change of the negative balance between the forces toward and away from the Jewish group into a positive balance, the creation of loyalty to the Jewish group instead of negative chauvinism. We are unable to safeguard our fellow Jews or our growing children today against those handicaps which are the result of their being Jewish. However, we can try to build up a Jewish education both on the children's level and on the adult level to counteract the *feeling of inferiority* and the *feeling of fear* which are the most important sources of the negative balance.

The feeling of inferiority of the Jew is but an indication of the fact that he sees things Jewish with the eyes of the unfriendly majority. I remember how, as an adolescent, I was deeply disturbed by the idea that the accusation against the Jews as being incapable of constructive work might be true. I know that many Jewish adolescents growing up in an atmosphere of prejudice felt similarly. Today, a Jewish youth who has watched Palestine grow, is in an infinitely better situation. Whatever one's opinion about Zionism as a political program may be, no one who has observed closely the German Jews during the fateful first weeks after Hitler's rise to power will deny that thousands of German Jews were saved from suicide only by the famous articles of the *Jüdische Rundschau*,[3] with its headlines *"Jasagen zum Judentum"* ("Saying Yes to Being a Jew"). The ideas expressed there were the rallying point and the source of strength for Zionist and non-Zionist alike.

To counteract fear and make the individual strong to face whatever the future holds, there is nothing so important as a clear and fully accepted belonging to a group whose fate has a positive meaning. A long range view which includes the past and the future of Jewish life, and links the solution of the minority problem with the problem of the welfare of all human beings is one of these possible sources of strength. A strong feeling of being part and parcel of the group and having a positive attitude

---

[3] A Zionist periodical.

toward it is, for children and adults alike, the sufficient condition for the avoidance of attitudes based on self-hatred.

To build up such feeling of group belongingness on the basis of active responsibility for the fellow Jew should be one of the outstanding policies in Jewish education. That does not mean that we can create in our children a feeling of belongingness by *forcing* them to go to the Sunday School or *Cheder*. Such a procedure means the establishment in early childhood of the same pattern of enforced group belongingness which is characteristic of the psychological situation for the negative chauvinists and it is sure to create in the long run exactly this attiude. Too many young Jews have been driven away from Judaism by too much *Cheder*. Our children should be brought up in contact with Jewish life in such a way that phrases like "the person looks Jewish" or "acts Jewish" take on a positive rather than a negative tone. That implies that a Jewish religious school should be conducted on a level at least comparable to the pedagogical standards of the rest of our schools.

Organizationally, the group as a whole would probably be greatly strengthened if we could get rid of our negative chauvinists. Such an expulsion is not possible. However, we might be able to approximate more closely a state of affairs in which belonging to the Jewish group is based—at least as far as we ourselves are concerned—on the willingness of the individual to accept active responsibility and sacrifice for the group. In my opinion, Jews have made a great mistake in assuming that to keep a large membership one should demand as little as possible from the individual. Strong groups are not built up that way, but rather by the opposite policy. We could learn something here, for instance, from the Catholic group. Actually, demanding a spirit of self-sacrifice from the individual is far more likely to decrease self-hatred.

One final point deserves mention. Many Jews seem to believe that prejudice against the Jew would disappear if every individual conducted himself properly—this in spite of all indications that the two facts have but little inter-communication. Jewish parents are accustomed to stress more than do other parents the importance of appearing well in public. This emphasis is one of the origins of the over-sensitivity to the behavior of the fellow Jew that we have mentioned previously, and a source of endless self-consciousness and tension. The more the individual learns to see the Jewish question as a social problem rather than as an individual problem of good conduct, thus placing a double burden on his shoulders, the more he will be able to act normally and freely. Such a normalizing of the tension level is probably the most important condition for the elimination of Jewish self-hatred.

Reprinted from *Contemporary Jewish Record*, Vol. IV, No. 3, with the permission of the editors.

GUIDE TO "SELF-HATRED AMONG JEWS"

INTRODUCTION:

1. The literature of anti-semitism is enormous. The explanations are equally varied and fruitless. It doesn't help us to live happily and well as Jews, to be forever speculating on why we are disliked by others.
2. A more useful approach is Lewin's. As a psychologist he wants to know how the Gentile's attitudes toward us actually affect us, our pride, our confidence in our people and in ourselves. He wants to know what happens to the Jew when he tries to escape from the Jewish group, to his mind and to his character. Among other things, he wants to understand why so many Jews seem to hate Jews.
3. No American ever says: "That phrase, that custom, that book is too American." But many Jews say or feel often that "it is too Jewish." Why? These questions and those below pose the problems which Lewin's article attempts to solve. After you have studied the article and the portraits in this pamphlet, together with Namier's essay on the Jews, you should be able to clarify your own answers to these questions.
    A. What is the effect of anti-semitism on the Jews' mind and behavior?
    B. How in normal phychological terms, can we explain the often peculiar attitudes and characteristics of Jews?
    C. Can this knowledge lead us to improve, to normalize our attitudes and our position in the world?

QUESTIONS:

1. Why do we squirm when Jews are loud or aggressive in public? Why do we glow when Einstein, or Menuchin or Cardozo are recognized as Jews?
2. "Interdependence of fate" (p. 29). This expresses the fact which is at the basis of the right answer to question A. When Jews are persecuted in Poland, can the most assimilated or "accepted" American Jew afford to feel only an impersonal interest in the fact? Must he not recognize that at least in the eyes of the world "all Jews are brothers"? The fate of every Jew depends on the fate of all the others. German Jews discovered this fact painfully.
3. Why is an Englishman, if he is proud of the achievement of other Englishmen, not made exquisitely unhappy when a fellow countryman sins or merely errs?
4. Why do many Jews hope to "pass" as Gentiles; why do Jews love to hear approbation from prominent, or even not so prominent, Gentiles, from a lecture platform or the pulpit?

5. "To gain status" (p. 30). Explain this phrase. Give examples from your own experience with various groups such as fraternities, social clubs, synagogues, etc.
6. Why can a member of an "underprivileged group" not leave it? Give other examples than the Jews. (p. 30) (negroes, aliens, etc.).
7. What is "negative chauvanism"? To be a chauvinist is to overrate your people, your religion, your nation and to be ready to attack aggressively anyone who seems to offend the honor of your group, or to question its importance. Sometimes chauvinism can be a very unpleasant trait, but after all it is quite natural and is often only an overzealous loyalty. Negative chauvinism (a phrase Lewin coins) is really nature inverted. To be a negative chauvinist is to *underrate* your people, your religion, your nation and to be ready to attack aggressively anyone or any quality that seems most clearly to represent your group. Negative chauvinism is what Jews feel who try so desperately to cut the silver cord which ties them to the Jewish people that they are capable of hating themselves because they are Jews.

   Give some symptoms or examples of negative chauvinism, as for example:
   (a) Jews who restlessly move to non-Jewish neighborhoods. (Notice Dr. Steinberger who says he has tried to avoid "ghettoizing.")
   (b) Jews who are ashamed of Hebrew. Notice how Marian Sanders defiantly crossed out the Hebrew inscription in her Psalter.
8. (p. 32). Instead of resentment against the powerful majority group, instead of chauvinism directed against the persecutors, the Jew whose heart is torn by negative chauvinism turns on the persecuted, on his own weak Jews and vents on them his bitter disappointment at not being fully accepted as a member of the superior, majority, privileged group.
   (a) What does the Christian mean by the phrase "a Christian Gentleman?" Can you think of a Jewish equivalent? What was implied in term "Talmud Chochem?" What is implied in the term "Chalutz?" Notice that a mere translation (pioneer) doesn't begin to hit all the connotations. Notice, too, that this Jewish term evokes no negative feelings, no embarrassment.
9. Organization of under-privileged groups (p. 33).
   (a) The individual of the privileged group, since he wholeheartedly admires the ideals, standards and entrenched position of his group (England or America or Catholicism) tends to look up to the most completely English or American or Catholic individual in his group and to try to be like him. The individual of the under-privileged group, on the other hand, does not relish being associated with his group, essentially admires the

power and position of the majority group, and so looks up to them or to any of his own group who succeed in being least like a Jew or a negro or a servant or whatever the "despised" group may happen to be.

(b) Study some Jewish leaders in your own community. Are they deeply rooted in Jewish life and attitudes? Are any of them men or women who do not want to be especially associated with the Jewish people? Why do we choose leaders who try to escape us?

(c) Why has the development of Palestine (p. 35) brought back "many Jews who had lost contact with Judaism." Compare Brandeis, Sampter, Sanders.

10. What can be done about Jewish self-hatred?
    (a) What in general is Lewin's recommendation?
    (b) Can you enlarge on this or make it more specific?
    (c) Whatever tends to make the Jew value his people or group, Judaism or the quality of the Jewish group is of itself his best protection against the psychopathology of self-hatred. Notice the effect of the Zionist paper's positive stand on the Jews in Hitler's Germany (p. 36). Mere admiration for the past achievements of Jews may remain academic. Intimate knowledge of Judaism, its values and ideals, its language (Hebrew) and its literature change the personality, inspire confidence in the importance of the Jewish group, remove any danger that the Jews will be felt to be an inferior group. This "conversion" is concretized in Zionism, which implies the ability of the Jewish people to establish itself firmly and well, not only on the soil of its own land, Palestine, but in a manner worthy of its great tradition.

    (1) Because in Zion, Jewish life and the Jewish group is normalized, loses the character of a minority, under-privileged "guest" group.

    (2) Because there, Jewish heroes of the soil, of industry, of the professions create as Jews and give positive value and importance to their own group.

    (3) Because there, Jews are forging weapons for the conquest of poverty and injustice in their new forms of social organization. (The Kvutzah, the cooperatives, etc.).

    (4) Because there, those great religious and ethical values, by which over half the world lives today, can again function and be revitalized. They are no longer confined in the covers of a book. They become again intimate aspects of Israel's life, to be shared by Israel all over the world. Witness the revival of Hebrew even in the Diaspora,

among a selected few, indeed—but these are the nucleus for teaching and spreading Hebraism. Hebrew is now taught in the high schools of New York and Chicago, and in colleges in New York and some other universities. It ceases to be merely an ancient grammar; it becomes a living language. Witness, too, the revival of Jewish music, drama and art through the connection with Palestine; the revitalization of festival observance, stemming from new forms created in Palestine.

(5) Thus, the rejuvenation of Israel in Eretz Yisrael as a real group and as a symbol of Jews everywhere can guarantee to all of us freedom from self-hatred to the extent that we identify ourselves with Eretz Yisrael and with the movement of Zionism.

COLLATERAL READING
BRINGING UP THE CHILD,
By KURT LEWIN
Menorah Journal, Vol. XXVIII, No. 1.

THE SOURCES

THE MAN IN A QUANDARY
In
"FROM MANY LANDS"
By Louis Adamic

When I first met him, Dr. Steinberger was forty three, but seemed younger in spite of his baldness; a lean man of medium height, with good posture and easy movements. Although far from handsome in the more conventional sense, he impressed one as being very attractive. His personality, though finely restrained, was independent, vivid, open, capable of varied expression. But there was a subtlety in its independence and openness, as there is in strong clear colors. Between the rather prominent ears, his clean-shaven, small face, with its lively brown eyes, held firmly a delicate balance between sardonic amusement and an uncertain, palpitating sadness.

Like many Jews, he did not "look Jewish"; indeed, his physiognomy could have been attributed to any of a dozen or more elements included in the American population. He was not Jewish in religion; and I discovered that I was familiar with items of Jewish history and lore he did not know, and that he was a Jew— intensely, self-consciously, with a peculiar interlacement of pride and discomfort-for the same reasons most other Jews I knew were Jews.

One evening, curious what he would say, I asked him, "Why are you a Jew?" He looked at me quizzically for a moment without replying. "I mean: what makes you a Jew?" "Well," he smiled, "I know I am a Jew, I just am; and—to put it awkwardly —I know that, because I just am and because, therefore, in one way or another, nearly every non-Jew draws a superficially or deeply cut line between himself and me, which underscores the fact that I am a Jew." He told me that when he entered a room in which there were Gentiles he knew with a basic, inevitable awareness that everybody there thought or soon would think of him as a Jew, and that-somehow-was important .

While not lacking in charm and other compensations, life in Baden was even then set and channelized and marked by special restrictions for the Jews; so at twenty, in 1863, Henry, Eliot's father—who, as he soon amply demonstrated, had within him the makings of an empire builder—left for America.

Henry Steinberger became president and actual directing head of the S. & S. itself, and also president of the Arctic Transportation Company, the West-East Live-Stock Transport Company, and a half-dozen other large enterprises. He was financially interested in several steamship companies which had installed refrigeration systems in their vessels on his urging. In the late 1900's and early 1910's, soon after it became known as Steinberger & Sons, the company grossed more than $100,000,000 annually.

His original nationality, he held, was German. Of course he was also a Jew; not a very religious but a very conscious one who made liberal donations to Jewish charities. He was the financial mainstay of a large hospital in New York and of a number of other institutions. Twice widowed, he married three times, each time a girl of German-Jewish stock. Friday evenings candles were lit in his home. On Saturdays he refrained from smoking; this, not only because me was a Jew who wanted to observe the Sabbath, but to test and exercise his will.

With all the power and money at his command, his life was shot through with a feeling of insecurity. The Jew in him? Perhaps. Most of the time he seemed to feel threatened. He inclined to expect the worst, and much of his thought and general energy went toward establishing a continuous series of systematic precautions.

Henry Steinberger remarried a year after the death of his first wife, and the second Mrs. Steinberger had five sons and three daughters. All were educated in private schools and foremost universities in America and Europe: Yale, Harvard, Vassar, Heidelberg, Sorbonne, Vienna. One has become a devout Catholic and almost entered the orders; his closest friend now is the priest in a little town in eastern Connecticut. Another is a Christion Scientist . . . Except for Louis, they are all married;

some to Jews, others to Gentiles. For years one of the daughters has been on the verge of Anglicizing her name; she is intensely and miserably anti-Semitic.

Eliot was the oldest of the third group of children. A tiny, unimportant figure in the big Steinberger story, he came to boyhood in the years immediately preceding the peak of his father's success as an industrialist.

Eliot was fear-ridden generally. He had frequent feelings of imminent disaster and death. Also, Eliot learned early that he was a Jew. This was all right in a way, something mysterious and wonderful, in fact, to be proud of at home, but something, too, for which the world unaccountably made you suffer.

Filled with questions and ever alert, the boy's mind worked all the time, trying to understand situations, people and things, and partly in consequence of this he developed into something like a prodigy.

The last year in private school he kept mainly to himself, joining no clubs, taking part in no group activities. He wanted to be different, aloof from the disquieting normality of the others. At fifteen, when he discovered his father did not think he belonged in the meat industry, he asked, then demanded, he be allowed to learn "the business from the ground up." This was in 1910. Surprised and pleased, Henry Steinberger, Sr.—now in his late sixties—let Eliot come into the plant.

Eliot plunged into learning the packing business with great determination. As soon as he mastered the various jobs and functions in one department, he was moved on to the next. The superintendents and foremen were delighted with him, and sought and made opportunities to tell the Big Boss how well his son was getting along.

At sixteen, from the slaughterhouse, Eliot advanced to the office, where he went swiftly through the various departments —stock, inventory, sales and orders, bookkeeping and billing, and research.

Eliot finally decided that the scientific end of the business interested him most. He began to spend nearly all of his time in the research department, of which the Old Boy was himself the directing head.

Meantime, a number of things in Eliot's life were converging on a common point from which he flew off on a tangent directly opposite to the tendencies he had begun to reveal in the plant and the office. Overdeveloped mentally for his sixteen years, emotionally unstable, and turning gradually into an attractive male despite his lack of what usually passes for good looks, he fell in and out of love a few times, mostly with women twice his age. This brought on sharp ups and downs in mood, and he became acutely dissatisfied with himself; with being a rich man's son and a Jew (for he bumped into mild forms of anti-Semitism every once in a while); with the packing business; with life at home; with things in general. He took to writing poetry, to contemplating human existence cynically. Despite his stature, the Old Boy began to strike him as a little ridiculous. This importance attached to meat and fats, to refrigeration!

Late in 1911, Louis, his favorite brother, came on a visit to New York, and he and Eliot had a talk. Eliot told him how he felt about things. Louis said, "Why don't you quit?" Reluctant to hurt the Old Boy, however, and thereby upset his mother, Eliot did not know for a while how to go about quitting. Meantime, Eliot, not yet seventeen, ran around and drank in earnest; and when he next met his father, he was drunk and bruised. He had engaged in a cafe brawl with a fellow who had called him "a dirty-rich Jew"; however, he declined now to explain the bruises to his parents. Eliot's step was a blow to the Old Boy. But he continued to be gentle to him and tried vainly to understand him.

Finally his father succeeded in catching him in a sober moment, and asked him to accompany him on a trip to Sioux Falls, where he was going on business. Eliot went along, and the two had a talk.

Eliot said, that "this fact of being a Jew" bothered him a great deal. His father did not reply for a long moment, and his face looked very heavy. Then he remarked slowly, as though it pained him to speak, that being a Jew was "a complicated business," hard to understand and harder to explain, but that maybe things would gradually improve, at least in the United States, with its democracy and attachment to fair play. The only thing Jews could do about it, he said, was to strive toward being the best sort of people, decent and progressive, in whatever field they might develop their activities. Some of the Jews were not trying any too hard, and one could not blame them (the worst of them were no worse than the worst of the Gentiles); however, they did make it hard on Jewry as a whole, for the Jews, as a group and as individuals, were watched by the rest of the human race—the poor conduct of one reflected on them as a group.

"But *why* are we watched?" demanded Eliot angrily.

The expression of his father's face became even heavier. He seemed unable to answer in a way that could satisfy the boy, the intensity of whose gaze cut into him. He said it all seemed a matter of history, tradition, and the ways of the world.

"What makes us Jews?" asked the young man.

"We just *are* Jews, that's all," returned the old man, unsatisfactorily. "I can't tell you why."

They fell silent.

"But this is neither here nor there," the Old Boy said, wanting to change the subject. He asked Eliot what he thought he wanted to do now. Eliot did not know. The old man suggested he go on with his schooling. How about Harvard? Of course they might not take him. Why not? Because Harvard's requirements were very stiff, especially for Jewish boys; the number of Jews they took in was limited. Involuntarily, the elder Steinberger had returned to the Jewish question, which Eliot promptly took up. *Why* did Harvard limit the number of Jewish students? The Old Boy replied, "It's part of the same thing you asked me about awhile ago. I can't explain it, son; I'm sorry."

Eliot felt challenged; and by the time they returned from Sioux Falls, they decided—holding one another in mutual respect again—that he would "try" Harvard.

Eliot applied for entrance to a small, exclusive preparatory school in Boston which annually "prepared" for Harvard from ten to a dozen sons of prominent, well-to-do families who lacked the necessary entrance credits.

One day he overheard a couple of boys talk about him. They said they liked him, he was a nice fellow, and all that; but wasn't it too bad, remarked one, that he was a Jew. Why? asked the other. Because it was difficult, said the first boy, for Jews to get into Harvard; and if Eliot did get in, they would be unable to associate with him on close terms. He would not be "available" for membership in this and that. Why? asked the second boy. Because he was a Jew, said the first; his father was a Jew; his name was Jewish . . . .

This conversation pierced Eliot like a rusty dagger. But after the first overwhelming feeling of anger and pain it acted as a further stimulus for his determination. He became even more aloof and studied still harder. Harvard Yard was a citadel to be taken.

He took it . . . and enjoyed his victory awhile. Then the thrill wore off, and he decided he did not like Harvard. He could not bring himself to study. His father was giving him a generous allowance, he had a car, and he resumed drinking and carousing. He went out with a small group of students, the majority of them Gentiles, who were regular (or, rather, *ir*regular) fellows and regarded themselves as "bums," scorning the general social life of the students.

There was a Jewish group, clique, but Eliot steered clear of it, with this thought in his head: why should he become part of the Jewish group simply because he was Jewish (whatever being Jewish was supposed to mean)? He was thinking over the conversation of the two boys in the "prep" school and what his father had said to him on the subject of being a Jew. It was all a great puzzle; where could one begin to unravel it? Some Jews "looked Jewish"; others did not. He, himself, for one, did not. So what made him a Jew? His name? The accident of being the son of a man named Steinberger? He was an American; no? Was he or wasn't he? He was born here. He was a citizen. In a few years he would be able to vote. His father was a citizen. The Old Boy's function reached deep into the existence of the country. If all this didn't make him an American, what could? What made anybody else an American? Assuming he was a Jew, why should that interfere with his being an American? Why should *he* get it in the neck because some Jews were not what some of the Gentiles thought they should be, while individual Gentiles (which apparently meant simply being non-Jewish) and Gentiles as a whole did not suffer the consequences of the misdeeds, crimes, and bad manners of Gentiles who were not everything they should be according to the standards which the Gentiles applied to Jews? . . . Eliot's head whirled. He thought his father's ideas on these questions were most unsatisfactory. "History," "tradition." Why should he have to try to be "the best sort of person" because he was a Jew? He resented that requirement and every impulse in him went against any effort toward meeting it; and, trying to puzzle things out, he felt his brain reeling in confusion. He was at once intensely and vaguely uncomfortable.

This discomfort increased. While there was no open, active anti-Jewish sentiment at Harvard, Jews were merely (but very definitely) not accepted, not really taken in, particularly by the New Englanders, who seemed to be the majority and the dominant element in the student body. They were unfailingly polite to him (as they were to all ather Jews), but he was essentially "out," not of them and there seemed to be an unwritten law that he never could be. He noticed that when he or some other Jewish student approached a group of old-stock Americans, they fell silent or abruptly changed the subject to some innocuous topic. Jews could occasionally go out drinking with them, but not appear where they might meet their girls, families and close friends.

Eliot perceived that Jews were virtually forced (quite apart from their own impulses in that direction) to congregate in a clique of their own; but he would be damned, he said to himself, if these perfect-mannered New England snobs would drive *him* into it! He continued to go out with the "bums," drinking with them, taking part in their escapades.

Then he learned that, on account of his unsatisfactory behavior and utter indifference to what the college had to offer him, he would be asked to leave, or be dropped or expelled; and so—sick not only of Harvard, but everything including himself—he just left his dormitory room one afternoon, carrying only a little bag into which he had thrown some of his belongings, and never went back. To the devil with Harvard.

Reaching the family house in New York, Eliot learned from the housekeeper that his father was very ill and on the way to a sanitarium in Europe with his mother and the younger children. The housekeeper gave him his family's address in Europe, and he walked out of the house with this thought trembling in his brain, "I don't want anything more from the family till I find out if I can stand on my own . . . Till I see if I can make something of myself, not because I am my old man's son or this mysterious thing called a Jew, but just on general principles, because I am what I am."

Eliot pawned his expensive watch, then bought a steerage passage on a ship sailing for Hamburg the next day. In those days no passports were necessary.

When Eliot had lived in the Lower Depths for about two months (in England), his mother wrote him that his father was "a little better, thank God"; and into the large linen envelope containing this welcome message she had stuffed a wad of thousand-franc notes. So now, with the autumn coming on, he abruptly bought himself a wardrobe, including silk shirts, and moved into the Savoy Hotel, feeling an irresolute weakling, a backslider for using the family money and violating the resolution he had made before leaving New York, while in the same flow of thought he told himself that the sordidness of the slums had become intolerable, and he needed a taste of this other life, lest he go crazy.

Assuming on the basis of his mother's last letter that his father was recovering, Eliot decided to drop out of Bill Bond's life and made for Marseilles, where he took ship for Australia—a long, pleasant trip by way of Suez and India. He chose Australia because he wanted to put distance between his family and himself.

Landing in Adelaid penniless, he starved for a week . . . till he landed a job with a large British sheep and wool firm, which had stations and vast herds throughout the interior of South Australia and also in Queensland, New South Wales, and Western Australia.

Claiming to be a good horseman (on the basis of a half-dozen rides in Central Park in New York City a few years before), Eliot was hired as a boundary rider, and was sent to a station "up beyond Innamincka," wherever that was. The place had no name, only a number—No. 9. His pay was to be a pound a week in cash and food supplies, and he was given a small advance to enable him to put a few meals under his belt before he set out for his post, and to purchase some toilet articles which were not procurable "in the Bush."

At the beginning, however, he had some difficulty cooking food so it was edible. The first week he all but starved. The vile-smelling ants attacked his meat sack, which he had hung by a rope on a limb of one of the few trees near the waterhole. He drank the filthy liquid which was supposed to be water or tea only when thirst became intolerable. This, on top of the long and strenuous trip to reach No. 9, reduced him to skin and bone. The second week, however, Eliot bounced into a new attitude.

At the end of the second week, a pack train, which continued on its way to a couple of locations farther on, brought him his next half-month's food supplies and firewood . . . and so it went for eight months, during which time Eliot had moments of feeling fairly sure he was meeting the test. He did not need the cushion of his family's wealth, nor the stimulus of being a Jew. Here, at eighteen, going on nineteen, he was a man on his own, doing a tough job satisfactorily, and getting paid for it. This realization made him rub his sun-bleached soft beard with mounting self-satisfaction and confidence. Now he could go anywhere, do almost anything.

At Harvard, and through most of his life prior to college, he had found it difficult to pick up a book, start reading it, and finish it. He had little use for magazines and newspapers. Now, by the faint light of a primitive lamp of his own invention, consisting of a piece of rag in a metal dish filled with mutton tallow, he read over and over again the scraps of paper in which his supplies had been wrapped. Then he began to ask the men of the pack train to bring him reading matter, and he perused anything and everything. Books were scarce in Innamincka, but, along with some pure trash, he got hold of a few by Kipling, which he liked for their vigor; and *The Jungle,* which he devoured with an interest verging on the personal, both representing and approving it; and, strangely enough, a little volume entitled *The Discourses of Keidansky* by Bernard G. Richards, published in New York in 1903, after most of it had appeared in the form of articles in *The Boston Evening Transcript*.

It is a book about Jews, and particularly about Jews in the Russian- and Polish-Jewish section in Boston at the turn of the century. Keidansky is an immigrant intellectual and a curious duck living in that section, maintaining a precarious existence as a journalist. He is somewhat of a socialist, and radical, but not really; a Zionist, but not really; and several other things, but none of them really. He is primarily a wit and eccentric (and there is room for argument if he is that), with opinions on nearly everything under the sun, but especially on the Jews, about whom he speaks from the inside. If he is nothing else, he is certainly a Jew. The chapter on "What Constitutes The Jew" interested Eliot most.

"What constitutes the Jew? For, of a verity, he is so complex in his character, so heterogeneous in his general composition, so diverse in his activities, so many sided in his worldly and heavenly pursuits, so widely varying in his appearance, so wonderfully ubiquitous, and withal such a living contradiction, that even after we have made the above painful efforts to understand him, we are still at a loss to know—what we know about him.

"He represents one of the ancient (groups of humanity) . . . and yet is up to date as any; he reaches deepest into the past and looks furthest into the future; he is the narrowest conservative and most advanced radical; in religion he is the most dogmatic, sectarian, stationary, orthodox, and also the most liberal and universal reformer; he is a member of the feeblest and strongest people on earth; he has no land of his own and he owns many lands; his wealth is the talk and the envy of the world, and none is so poor as he; his riches have ever been magnified and exaggerated, his dire poverty overlooked. 'As poor as a Jew' would be a truer simile than the one now in use. He is the infamous Shylock, the money-lender, yet he borrows as much and more money than he lends to others, only he pays his debts and so there is no talk about it; Christians and others who borrow from him go to court, denounce him, call him Shylock, and give him several pounds of 'tongue,' though he asks not for flesh, because it is not 'kosher,' and because whatever he is, he is never cruel.

"Now he is exclusively confined to his own Hebrew religious lore, believing that beyond it there are no heights to scale, no depths to fathom, and then he becomes a Georg Brandes, a great interpreter of the literatures of the world; his own literature is so Puritanical, so religious and chaste that there is hardly a single love song to be found therein, and then comes a Heinrich Heine. He is the slave of traditions and the first to break them; persecute him and he will die for the religion of his fathers; he is intensely religious and the rankest infidel; there is no one so clannish and so cosmopolitan as he is . . . and these contrasts can be multiplied to the abuse of time and space.

"If, then, he is everything and to be found anywhere, to be seen in all sorts of circumstances, in all walks of life and walking in so many diverse ways, making his way in such strongly contrasting conditions, how shall we know him?

"His isolated, peculiar and purely religious life, 'the spiritual Palestine,' which he has carried along with him in his wanderings through the darkness and cold of the Ghettos, has under all circumstances and in all the hazards preserved those fine domestic and social qualities for which he is noted. What can *now* be said about his domesticity, his love of home and care of his family; his sobriety, thrift, peacefulness and good deportment, the readiness with which he cares for his poor, his public spirit in the interest of his community—wherever that may be—his unequalled kindness . . . would be mere repetition; but these are nevertheless some of the undisputed qualities which constitute the Jew.

"The Jew is a great possibility. Sensitive of any susceptibility to all things, to the very color of the atmosphere around him with a soul sharpened by sorrow and a mind of keenest understanding, he can become anything and everything, assimilate himself with any and all conditions, and illustrate life with a new meaning or adorn it with a worthy work . . . ."

Along with the rest of Keidansky those words filled Eliot Steinberger, when he first read them, with a mingling of almost unbearable grief and profound peace. After spending eight months as a boundary rider, Eliot was assigned to a camel team in charge of an Afghan, whom everybody called Buffalo Bill.

Thirty-odd camels carried the large bales of wool from the station and the shearing sheds on some of the outposts to the far-off railroad sidings. Till he learned it thoroughly, this new work was dangerous. The camels were very erratic as well as extremely enduring beasts; and the trips through the Bush, most of them requiring from two to three weeks, often strained his spirit and every fiber of his physical being. But he met the requirements of his job, and a little more. One day a twitch of an approving smile flashed across Buffalo Bill's dead-pan Oriental face; it filled Eliot with a light that glowed for days.

Satisfied at last that he had passed the test, Eliot abruptly decided to quit his job. Without being in any great hurry about it, he thought he might return to the United States, and made his way to Melbourne with about fifty pounds to his name and the conviction that the thirteen months in the Bush had done him a universe of good.

Reaching the Golden Gate, Eliot Steinberger was penniless again. He went to work on the docks and earned his trainfare to Chicago, where—dressed as a workingman, without necktie and socks—he all but fought his way through the cordon of bellhops in the ornate lobby of the Palmer House to the desk, and demanded he be announced at once to his half brother, Louis Steinberger, who chanced to be in his suite there.

Louis was popeyed with delight listening to his young half brother's account of himself since his disappearance. In turn, he gave Eliot the news about the family and the S. & S. Both were in a bad way. The Old Boy was not expected to live through the summer. He was still in Switzerland, as were his (Eliot's) mother and brothers and sister.

Eliot sent a long cable to his mother, who replied begging him to come to Europe at once if he wished to see his father, who was asking for him. Within a few days he was on the way over . . . but five days out he received a wireless: *Father died last night.*

In February the United States severed its relations with Germany. To Eliot the European War had been at first a colossal stupidity; then as he followed the events and caught glimpses of the ideas behind them, his sympathies had become strongly pro-Ally.

Recognized as a first-rate instructor in flying, and against his repeated protests, Eliot was kept in the various air-training camps in the United States. Finally, he got over in the fall of 1918—too late to see combat action.

Less than a year after the Armistice, his mother and sister and brothers decided to return to Switzerland to live. In 1922, Eliot received a cable from his sister Ann: his brother Marshal had been killed in a fall from a horse. His mother was heartbroken, and Ann begged him to join them abroad at once.

Soon after Eliot got to Switzerland in 1922, his sister Ann, an exceptionally pretty and brilliant girl in love with a young Swiss who adored her, became afflicted with a serious case of acne, which in the next few years, in spite of all the efforts of medical science, ruined her lovely complexion and naturally affected her life drastically—a story all by itself, which I shall not even try to summarize here.

Her physician was Dr. Maxim Laubach of Zurich, a leading skin specialist with a volatile, hot passion for his profession. Eliot came to like him enormously. When he talked with him, or watched him treat Ann, or listened to him talk to her, he had a feeling he could define only as inspiration. The *Herr Doktor* was then already past middle age, a small man but tireless; a Jew with a bespectacled face, which flashed with quick, at once sad and humorous smiles, and seemed to accept the world in toto and with a fierce determination and a personal plan to help make it better.

In a few months Doctor Laubach and Eliot became deep friends.

Both because of Ann's tragic affliction and through her physician, Eliot became profoundly interested in medicine, and particularly in dermatology, as a science and practice. All at once he forgot himself. Without realizing it, he ceased asking what to do with himself. There were questions bigger than he and outside of him, inviting him to discover their answers. It was like no other challenge before. Listening to Doctor Laubach, he lost himself and found himself in the warmth of a great love, an enduring absorption.

The scholastic record which had admitted Eliot to Harvard was not sufficient in the judgment of the renowned medical school in Zurich, whose requirements were extremely high. Besides, his Harvard record weighed heavily against his enrollment. But Doctor Laubach, a member of the faculty, helped him to enter in 1923 . . . whereupon he studied "like hell" through most of the ensuing five years, as he had studied in the "prep" school in Boston 'way back in 1911-12; only with a different motive and spirit—not to take the citadel of Harvard, which limited the number of Jews, but to be a doctor, a fellow and brother of men like Maxim Laubach. The third year he began to be considered the most brilliant student in the school.

This development resolved one of his main dilemmas.

But the rest of the inner drama of his quandary continued. Most of the time he lived in extremely modest student quarters in a poor section of Zurich and watched with deep interest the ways and problems of the people in the neighborhood, feeling himself part of it. Then of a sudden, a powerful impulse would take him to St. Moritz, Monte Carlo, Nice or the Lido; where he took rooms in the most expensive hotels.

In 1925, at St. Moritz, he met Peggy Bryce, a beautiful young divorcée of old stock American ancestry, well-off, traveled, and constantly trailed by a squad of love-smitten males of various ages. At thirty-one Eliot was already bald (a family trait), but this did not diminish his attractiveness; and Peggy, bored by the attentions of the conventional playboys and would-be playboys who never pierced her intelligence, found him stimulating and agreeable company. He was moved to write poetry again and excel himself in love-making.

In the next few years, as a medical student, Eliot kept in touch with Peggy, who was increasingly fascinated by him. He sent her his poems. Every four or five months they met at St. Moritz or the Lido and had joyous times for a week or two at a spell. Then they quarreled and parted.

They could not shake one another out of their respective make-ups; but his quandary, her high-strung temperament and the hangover of her first marriage, the fact that he was a Jew and she a Gentile, and diverse intangibles which stemmed from the other factors and intermingled, producing endless absurd but extremely real difficulties, kept them from marrying. Both their families objected to the affair: his, on the ground that she was a Gentile, a divorcée, a woman of the world; hers, that he was a Jew. This crossfire of objections caused nasty scenes on both sides, with unpleasant repercussions in the middle.

Eliot became once more aware that he was a Jew. From a secondhand bookshop in New York he procured another copy of *Keidansky,* then re-read again the chapter on "What Constitutes the Jew?" It once more simultaneously exalted and depressed him, and these complex "Jewish moods," as he subsequently recalled them, no doubt influenced his love affair.

He made her angry, furious. There was a continual tension between them, simultaneously pleasant and unbearable. She wondered: was this part of "the Jew-Gentile business"? Was he so damnably interesting because he was a Jew? She did not know; she had had distant contacts with a few Jews who seemed rather dull; but she inclined to think that in Eliot his being Jewish had a great deal to do with his being interesting. One day in the seventh or eight year of their tumultuous relationship he asked her to read his favorite chapter in *Keidansky.*

"Why," she exclaimed, "this is you all over!"

By-and-by, as they both grew older and started to realize how inevitable "this whole thing" was, the difficulties between them began to melt away. Their families gradually ceased to object . . . And finally, in 1936, when he was already an established doctor in New York, they married, puzzled why they had not done so before; and their private life—full of stimulating tensions, most of them springing from his quandary and her high-strung temperament—has been very much of a mutual success.

Eliot passed his "State exam" in 1930 and, toward the end of that year, opened his office in the Seventies off Park Avenue. By 1933 he was widely recognized as a "coming man" in the field. He had already published a number of papers in the United States, Germany, Switzerland and France, and was being asked to talk before medical societies. He became a lecturer in a medical school in New York City. He published his first book. He was obliged to move to a larger office.

In May, 1940, he could barely be restrained from offering his services as a flyer to the Allies. It was difficult for him to continue looking objectively at what he saw; it was hard for him to stand

and do nothing. He responded as a Jew, a numan being, an American who believed in Democracy, suffering "every blow and kick delivered by every Gestapo agent at every prisoner, Jew or Gentile, in every concentration camp." When he said this to me, one day early in 1939 the curious expression on his face wontedly so finely balanced between amusement and near-despair abruptly turned all agony, and he "looked Jewish."

One of the most frequent subjects of discussion between him and me was the idea, on which we essentially agreed, that there really was no "Jewish problem" as something apart from the American and general human problem. He said that anti-Semitism was but a symptom of the disease he considered dangerous. Both of us held that "we would have to get together, somehow, soon," all of us who came or stemmed from the many lands of the Old World, who were Gentiles and Jews, white and black and yellow and red, Polish, Welsh, Irish, Slovenian, Americans, etcetera, to acquire an insight into one another. But how to do that? So many elements of the American people set themselves apart. On an occasion a friend of mine who happened to be in the conversation addressed a remark to Eliot Steinberger that there was basis for the oft-heard statement that the Jews were clannish.

"I dislike to merely defend the Jews," he replied, " . . . but my impression, stating it as objectively as I can, is that their clannishness is, roughly, one-third a matter of their own impulse and making, a result of their desire to hang together communally and otherwise, and two-thirds imposed upon them by the attitudes toward them of the non-Jews. I married a Gentile, I mingle with Gentiles, and want to mingle with them much more and on a much more natural and agreeable basis than I do; but consider this: For years Peggy, a Gentile afflicted with the name of Steinberger, had difficulty in renting houses for our summer vacations. She was refused as a would-be-tenant in Greenwich, Connecticut, on Cape Cod, and elsewhere; and finally we had trouble finding people willing to sell us a summer place which was not in a Jewish community. I resisted the pressure to drive me into Jewish clannishness at Harvard; I have been resisting it in New York and elsewhere in recent years—successfully, so far, perhaps only because I am more advantageously placed than are most Jews.

Most of them cannot cope with it. They become clannish . . . How long will I hold out? . . . I am supposed to be a fairly well-known doctor, but before I enter the home or hospital room of any of my influential or well-known or very wealthy Gentile patients I look at myself in a mirror if I have the chance, to make sure about my appearance. If there is no mirror, I examine myself as well as I can without it. I feel my necktie to make sure it is straight. All this because I am a Jew. I am conscious that I am on trial; not only I, myself, but Jews—"

As I write these concluding paragraphs of his story (in July, 1940), Eliot Steinberger's quandary continues with fluctuating confusing emphases on his various predicaments.

How to be free and strong in a world of others who also would be free and strong, but who, like oneself, are weak and pulling and clawing at one another. In other words, how to end this pointless struggle?

"It's easy to ask these questions and to criticize humanity. To do something about it is another matter." He smiled, relaxing for a moment the intensity of his dark eyes. "I can't be consistently objective myself. I get in my own way, let others get in my way."

"How?" I asked.

"Well, in my work as a doctor for example, I am not doing ten per cent of what I could do."

"Why? What do you mean—specifically?"

He shrugged and smiled again. "Well, let us say I am called into a consultation with Gentile doctors. What happens? Both they and I are aware of what I am: a Jew. This mutual consciousness not only stands between us, but between us and the case. Often, of course, I have nothing to contribute; sometimes I have. Sometimes I am afraid if I offer something my Gentile colleagues do not know there will be resentment against me as a Jew and against the Jews generally. Of course I speak out anyhow. But, in nine cases out of ten, I am not entirely free to give the best in me—everything I say is just a little distorted by the fact that I am a Jew; not necessarily in content, but the way I say it. There is nearly always this fear: if I am too right or too prophetic, it may create a feeling not only against me but against Jews. If I am wrong, this will be remembered and magnified because I am a Jew. Occasionally I have, or think I have, clear evidence in the facial expression and manner of Gentile physicians that they fear that I, a Jew, may have some part of the answer they don't have; even though, as non-dermatologist, they could not be expected to have it . . . . By this I do not mean to criticize my Gentile colleagues any more than I mean to criticize myself. In fact, myself more than them; or rather, neither. What I really want to say is that the consciousness of my being a Jew and therefore on trial more than the Gentiles and bearing additional responsibility both for myself and for all other Jews, is always with me to a greater or lesser degree and is often accentuated in certain circumstances such as a consultation with eminent and eminently non-Jewish fellow doctors. Then I (but usually no one else) become aware of certain strains and inhibitions which prevent me from being my natural self; I am conscious of being either too timid or too aggressive—in short, not myself. I don't know whether I am more or less efficient, better or worse, because of this feeling of discomfort and added responsibility . . . . This feeling is probably both beneficial and detrimental, sometimes acting as a spur or as stabilizer and sometimes acting as an impediment, according to the situation and/or the temperament of the individual.

"In 1931 I was in line for promotion to a leading position on a hospital staff; I was frankly told, 'We already have two Jewish chiefs of departments,' and they took on a Gentile because he was a Gentile. Two years later I became dissatisfied with my opportunities for the studying and teaching of dermatology; I thought of trying to get a teaching job in a small medical school which might lead to a four-or-five-thousand-dollar-a-year professorship, and which might enable me to really delve into dermatology as a science in collaboration with specialists in other fields in medicine, and train young doctors. I discovered I did not have a chance . . .

"But this may sound like bellyaching. Really, I am not talking only about myself, about Jews. We agree; there is no 'Jewish problem.' Anti-Semitism is but one symptom. I know a brilliant Negro doctor in Harlem and another brilliant doctor who was born in Oregon of Japanese parents; their chances are slimmer than mine; they are not doing *two* percent of what they could do . . . .

"The waste of it! I think I probably feel," he smiled, "as my father felt back in the 1860's and '70's contemplating the waste in the butcher trade. Only the problem of the waste that bothers me is much more complex than was the one that drove him to rendering fat into tallow and oleomargarine . . ."

Several sentences in his copy of *The Discourse of Keidansky,* which he let me read, are pencil-marked. There is a specially emphatic line under the words, *"The Jew is a great possibility."*

I asked him about it.

He smiled, "I don't mean that only the Jew is a great possibility. Man—humanity is a great possibility.

"The Jew is perhaps an intensification of humanity, of its inner contradictions, its powers and weaknesses. The Jew is extreme in many ways, 'a graduate of sorrow *cum laude,*' and as such somewhat of an over-clear mirror of the human breed as a whole. As I have said, he is on trial. So is the rest of humanity; only it does not know it as clearly as he knows it. Therein is the source of his great discomfort, also his advantage over the non-Jew. He exerts himself more; he must be good . . . . If only man generally realized fully he was on trial!

"In part because man generally does not realize this as fully as the Jew, the Jew is uncomfortable. At many points he, himself, is anti-Semitic. He does not like his 'clannishness.' He is discontent whether he is rich or poor; if rich, because others are poor; if poor, because he lacks even the illusion of security which wealth sometimes provides, and so he wants it and, in some cases, is apt to do almost anything to get it. In this his predicament and disposition are the same as the average Gentile's; only more so.

"What are our prejudices, our contradictions and quandaries doing to us all? Why do we physicians labor and sacrifice our strength and our happiness and our lives to relieve suffering, and then see that others no different fundamentally from ourselves devote their minds and energies to the creation of suffering? Why are we, humanity in general, sick with hate, stalled, held back from creativity? What would be our possibilities—here in

America, in the world—if we freed ourselves of them, all of us?" He spoke in an even, quiet tone, but his whole being was aflame with these questions. "What if we ceased to be primarily Jews or X-ians and become primarily men? What if we became free agents, free to tackle the mysteries?" He smiled. *"That's* the great possibility that interests me."

GUIDE TO "DOCTOR STEINBERGER"

1. Is there any personal security in the family background? Compare the *normal* family, devoted Jewish parents, the sense of security a "Jewish" mother gives psychologically? (More often good than bad); the love and security root the person into a group background.

2. Is there any Jewish ideal, mode of life, idealism, devotion to a cause? Compare the lack of all group affiliation or ceremony or interpretation of Judaism in Eliot's home life. Notice his conversation with his father on the train to Sioux City. Their Judaism is only a racial burden.

3. Notice the restlessness and lack of any sense of belonging or values as reflected in the ups and downs of his life, his jumping from poverty to wealth and back again; his austerity, his poverty are pointless. (Compare work and austerity in Eretz Yisrael for a cause). Therefore, Eliot's poverty is always followed by carousing and extravagance.

4. The gifted man is finally galvanized by the ideal of medicine, but note that his search for security continues; he marries a Gentile, he avoids "Ghettoizing," though he is living with or near Jews. He continues supremely self-conscious in the presence of Gentile doctors where you would expect the professional relationship to supersede any sense of self.

5. Did wealth, personal success, professional achievement or his apparently successful assimilation through inter-marriage and friendship with Gentiles alleviate his restlessness or his sense of security as a Jew? Did even his joy in his career bring him complete self-fulfillment?

6. Are his relations with Gentiles in general easy, normal, man to man? Obviously not. He is usually apologetic, always self-conscious. His effort is directed at understanding the Jew, namely, still himself, but never the Jewish people or his relation to it. Thus he escapes the solution which implies the Jewish people, extending both in time and

in space. The Jewish problem is two dimensional: the individual is always a single dimension, himself, now.

7. Notice on top of page 64 Steinberger says, "What if we ceased to be primarily Jews or Christians and became primarily men." Amazing how a scientist can become unscientific as soon as he ventures into any field but his own! The only man who is primarily a man, and *not* an American, or a Jew, or a Catholic, is a wild man who has grown up in the woods away from other human creatures. And even *he* is hardly a *man*. Human beings are social beings. No person makes up his own language; he must learn it from a group. Therefore, it is necessarily not human language, but English, or French, or Hebrew. From his group, a man learns his ideas of what is right and what wrong, what is noble and what despicable. A man is a *mere* man. A Jew, a Socialist, a Democrat, a Quaker, is a man plus a group and therefore a man with ideas and ideals.

COLLATERAL READING

1. Read more of the biographies in *From Many Lands*, by Louis Adamic. Compare the adjustment of other immigrant groups to America with the Jewish.
2. *The Island Within*, by Ludwig Lewisohn. Notice Arthur Levy (the hero) and compare him with Dr. Steinberger.

"Man in a Quandary," condensed from Chapter I, *From Many Lands*, by Louis Adamic, by permission of Harper and Brothers.

MARIAN SANDERS' STORY
By
RUTH JONAS BARDIN

Marian was a beautiful baby, rosy, healthy, blue-eyed, golden-haired. Her chubby hands played with the sunbeams on her carriage cover. What more could she have wished for, thought her mother, Theresa Sanders. "I prayed for intelligence and she has beauty as well."

At five years, Marian played in the street with the neighbor children, or often they assembled for a game on her lawn. It was good wholesome play, with skipping-rope rhymes and jingled taunts, and excursions and the mulberry tree that, given a shake, would shed its juicy fruit into the childrens' upturned mouths. There was all the vernacular of the local scene. Marian was a healthy, happy-natured child and was accepted, for several years, as the leader of the gang on the block.

At about six, her friend Charles, from his porch across the street, would call tentatively and teasingly, "Your mother is a dirty Jew." Marian retorted cheerfully, "Yours is a dirty fat pig." Seasons came and went,—Christmas, Easter, St. Patrick's Day,—all the local color and the local customs. Marian still led the gang. Only now at six and a half she was introduced to school. Clutching the hand of her father, Fred Sanders, who was a never-failing source of comfort, she mounted the broad steps of the private school where she was to spend most of her waking hours, for many years ,among Gentile girls.

Marian learned very easily. Her classmates were pleasant, and visits were exchanged. But gradually, Marian became sensitive to an under-current of childish speculation about herself. She told her principal very gravely at about eight or nine years of age that she would like to be excused from chapel services since she was not a believer in his faith. She was not excused.

Marian loved drawing and crafts and literature. She revelled in Dickens and Scott and particularly in poetry. It was probably in the fourth grade that the class was reading the Psalms. Marian noticed the inscription in her little volume of Psalms, and took it to be Yiddish. She had never consciously heard that language but the strange characters were associated in her mind with all those subway journeys when her classmates' innuendoes had made her blush with shame both for the innocent old bearded Jews they were taunting and for the embarrassment she herself felt in being linked with these "outlandish" people. There was no escaping the girls' suspicions. When they asked her whether she was a Jewess, she really didn't know how to reply. She conceded, "My ancestors were Jews." But she called herself, at an absurdly precocious age, an "agnostic." No intelligent child could fail to realize that to be a Jewess, in her classmates' eyes, was to be very unwelcome. So when the girls turned and stared and pointed at those strange characters in the Psalm book and subtly implicated her in their foreign-ness, Marian, in desperation, struck out the words in heavy black ink lines! (It was only many years later that she learned those words were Hebrew!)

Marian knew, of course, that her great-grandmother was a Jewess, but stress had always been on German culture and backgrounds and the German language. Marian's teacher at school had praised the purity of her German pronounciation, and had inculcated in her pride in German achievements and in the mighty "fatherland." Great-grandmother took pride in Marian's German letters and conversations, and recitations. The old lady had come to Boston as a young girl and Marian was of the third generation born in America. Her father, Fred's family, also from Germany, found its diversion from the American scene in Plattdeutsch.

Therese Sanders, Marian's mother, had been brought up in Boston and was strongly influenced by New England puritanism, particularly by the writings of Ralph Waldo Emerson. She had come to Brooklyn as a young woman. Throughout her life she nurtured in herself a spiritual spark and a great strength of character.

Fred Sanders had grown up in Brooklyn among German-Americans, many of them non-Jews. He refused to recognize any inherent differences between Jew and Gentile. He was consistently and sincerely a "liberal." His familiarity with Jewish backgrounds was negligible. Neither he nor his son was Bar Mitzvah. But through his wide experience and human interests, Fred became aware of and remained tolerant of most of mankind's frailties. Only, in retrospect, it seemed to Marian that her father had leant over backwards to place the faults at the Jewish door and to justify the Gentile.

Fred's parents had had little or no interest in Judaism. He himself inclined toward devastating rationalism and intellectualism. A sentimentalist, he rhapsodized on the beauties of home and family life yet spent little time at home. A theorist, he avidly followed developments in internationalism, an international language, inter-faith relationships. Yet as far as Marian could tell, he had never probed his own relations with the despised group from which he derived.

Marian's patience was taxed by her parents' maxim, "A Jew must be twice as good and virtuous and studious and mannerly as a Gentile to pass at all." She was vaguely and, in a troubled sort of way, rebellious.

Both Marian's parents were members of the Ethical Culture Society and devoted followers of its founder, Dr. Felix Adler. This society drew electically from all religious teachings and served up its findings indiscriminately. The common basis of ethical obligations and relationships was the angle stressed. By thus pooling the world's spiritual and ethical heritage, a uniting rather than dividing religion would evolve and boundaries disappear.

Fred explained his own position thus. Marian (as well as his other children) was to be given no specific religious training, but was to be allowed to visit many churches, and, in time, to "choose a religion" as her own. As it worked out, the lonely little girl visited with classmates Swedenborgian, Congregationalist, Presbyterian, Quaker and Catholic churches. She loved the singing which she missed at the Ethical Culture Society meetings. But a weary sense of "not belonging" dogged her. As her mother put it, Marian was re-evaluating the world from A to Z. (And Theresa was definitely uneasy about it).

Theresa was a perfectionist and that philosophy necessarily assumes a progression, a series of stages toward a goal. Cut adrift from the traditional past, granted much freedom, perfection took on the form of absolute adherence to the ways and mores of the majority Gentile group. It resulted in harsh self-criticism, self-derision whenever one deviated, however slightly, from the accepted pattern. Now the friends of the Sanders' family were predominantly the same type of Jew as themselves. In many of them this pruning of themselves to fit the mold of the "others" bred a bitter self-hatred.

Marian rebelled. She was extremely literal in her acceptance of the teachings of those in whom she had faith. She recognized an evasion of the problems of non-acceptance of the Jews by the Gentiles, in the non-acceptance of the Jews by the Jews. Yet she was bewildered and saw no way out. But, she reckoned, if Dr. Adler, for example, was stressing ethical values in human relationships as over and above dogma, then it must be possible *to live* according to these principles and without incurring the scorn of one's worldly neighbors.

Marian did not look Jewish. She was generally taken for an English girl. Her family background, social and economic, was "desirable." Her father was careful to spread his generous philanthropies over several groups, giving at least as much to Catholic and to Negro groups as to Jewish. The very existence of the Hebrew holidays was unknown to Marian . . . even the High Holy Days. So that absence from school on religious grounds never occurred. But she knew she was Jewish, and so did her class-mates, and the knowledge, being carefully avoided in conversation, festered within her.

Some of Marian's friends were drawn to Communism, some to Catholicism. Had one said anything to her at that time about a national ethos, she would have squirmed uncomfortably and suspiciously. Yet the propaganda of young socialist minister B left her cold. She knew from experience that such equality was not for her nor for her ilk. There must be somewhere, somehow, something uniquely her and their own. Marian proceeded on a simple formula. What Marian eats becomes Marian. What Marian does not digest is not for Marian.

Why, you may ask, was she not drawn to one or another Jewish group in New York? Marian, in pain, had developed a defense mechanism to hide from herself any relationship with that "foreign "group. She had by now a complex sorting-machine which allowed only de-Judaized impressions of Jews to impinge upon her awareness. She perpetually felt the presence of the Gentile over her shoulder, criticizing her reactions, suspicious of the completeness of her assimilation. She could not simply like Jews ... she must, of necessity, albeit subconsciously, weigh the desirability of associating with such and such Jews.

The week preceding Christmas was always a happy one, tingling with excitement. There were meticulous preparations, making and purchasing of gifts, wrapping them attractively. When the younger children were in bed, her mother would allow Marian to help her hoist the tree in place. Nothing, in later life when Marian had renounced non-Jewish ways, was ever to replace for her the fullness of that experience, the sense of completion ... effort-making preparations, ritual and glow. Comparable to it, perhaps, was only the Seder, when Marian celebrated it, years later, with her husband and two sons; when they had scoured and scrubbed and feasted and mulled over the Haggadah. But at the time of which we are speaking Marian would have innocently asked, what is Pesach?

Marian's friend Alfred, who was the son of her mother's friends, would arrive late Christmas eve to spend his vacation from college with the Sanders family. Together the young people draped the gay festoons and green branches along the balustrade. They decked out the tree in all the childish finery and gaudiness held over from year to year. There were gifts under the tree, German songs (they loved to sing). Alfred was a musician and German songs were so melodious.

No single discordant note broke into the feeling of at-oneness, in emotion and celebration, with the surrounding community. True, Hannah, Theresa's friend and wife of a reform rabbi, demurred at the tree. (Yet, strangely enough in later years Hannah's grandchildren were to cling to the tree tradition and Theresa's grandchildren were Palestinians). The only discomfort was that, when the Irish maid entered the room at dinnertime, natural conversation became hushed and any mention of

Jews was transformed mysteriously to "Mexicans." It was, of course, typical ostrich-hiding-its-head-in-the-sand tactics! But this was so much a matter of habit that no one paid much attention to it.

When Marian was nineteen an opportunity presented itself to send the girl on a Mediterranean cruise. Theresa jumped at it. It was a series of intoxicating experiences for Marian who came to travel with the trained eye and ear of an artist. But the climax was the week spent in Palestine. To a "normal" Jew the complete naivete of the girl may seem unbelievable, yet Marian, though she knew she was a Jewess, knew nothing whatsoever of her place in the chronology of Jewish generations. Nor did Palestine have any Jewish significance to her. She had no inkling of her past or future connections with the Land. The cruise manager ingratiatingly pointed out all the holy places of the Gentile world. And Marian had no clue to Jewish interests there.

By the merest chance two young Zionists sat down at the table, in the Allenby Hotel in Jerusalem, where Marian and her chaperone were dining. She spoke German and they spoke Yiddish. They excited her curiosity thoroughly. "What," they exclaimed, "you a Jewess and don't know that Jews are settling here and working the land!" They whisked her off, two utter strangers, in the few hours before sailing time, through Jewish fields to a sea-side group of houses known then as "Tel Aviv." She sat in a little cafe trying to understand the "Yiddish" of the Jewish workers there. She did not know she was listening to Hebrew, Russian and Polish as well. She sensed here was a group of Jews, unconcerned about the outer world's favorable opinion. Marian had always been irked by the time wasted in negations and self-explanatory apologies. Here were sturdy workers whose only standards were Jewish standards.

Whizzing through the fields, they passed Arabs swathed in picturesque long robes, camels, goats and mules. By comparison the Jews looked normal and healthy. It was not sentimental sympathy for the picturesque that caught Marian and made her feel "at home." The shell of self-protective rejection of the Jews was smashed. Here no one watched her reactions, nor would she have cared if they had. Hands gesticulating in accompaniment of speech, warm Yiddishisms invading over-pure English and over-pure German . . . what an informal relief!

On her return to America, Marian horrified her family by declaring she would live in Palestine. She vouchsafed no explanation. It was too difficult to make others understand what she herself had just glimpsed. She was still unaware of the Hebrew language. Of all those who heard Marian's plan, only one encouraged her. He was an elderly gentleman who persuaded her to study Hebrew and even found her a teacher. It was a tremendous release to discover that, hidden behind those strange "Yiddish" characters which had made her suffer in her school-mates' presence, were the noble utterances of an ancient tongue.

At about this time Felix Adler invited Marian to spend a few days with him and his family in the mountains. He wrote reassuringly to Theresa, ". . . she is a fine girl and when the present transitional period in her life is past, she will make a splendid woman . . . whether she goes to Palestine or not is not the most important consideration. I have tried to impress on her that in looking to the Jewish group for her spiritual environment she is looking in the wrong direction. She has no strong Jewish feeling, is not interested in Zionism. She simply bears the marks of early contact with anti-Semitism. What she really craves is the society of kindred spirits and that she will have as soon as she has distinguished herself in her chosen vocation of art . . ." Marian did concentrate on painting and sculpturing, working professionally. She also wrote poetry and prose.

As she studied Hebrew and became aware of Zionism, it seemed crystal clear to Marian that what she had respected in Dr. Adler's teachings allowed of no other interpretation. That for herself, as a Jewess, the ethical way of life was positive living among fellow Jews, creating at every level of endeavor, in every kind of occupation. And it seemed to her that only in such a community as was there in Palestine could she satisfactorily test out that life and herself. For as long as she remained one of a scorned minority amidst an unfriendly majority, she spent her time explaining, negating, apologizing. *Could* she, after all, live positively? As an artist she would create best from within a group that accepted her. If only we could prove ourselves in

Palestine, all Jews everywhere would know it can be done. We can live a free creative life wherever we are.

In vain she asked advice of several New York rabbis. What was the essence of Judaism, how could she find her way back to a security and peace among her own folk? In the end she formulated it for herself. "Create out of yourself according to your own intuitions and you will be living as a Jewess." She banked on the belief that Jewishness was latent in her being. And yet, she was still far from acceptance of herself as a Jew. She still had moments of retrogression, of discomfort, of shutting out the unfamiliar idiosyncracies that grated on her self-consciousness.

Her second and decisive visit to Palestine came a few years later when she spent three intensely active months, getting acquainted with the Land, the people and herself amongst the people. She spoke Hebrew and German all day long. She was very happy. At last here was a community for her to live in. She prowled the streets eager to face Jews, with no mental reservations, caused by the Gentile-at-the-elbow sensation. She engaged women and old men and children in conversation, seeking to cram into the brief hours all the ease of communication which she had always denied herself. She no longer felt the compulsion to mirror the Gentile's distaste for the Jew. Here cooperative colonies and social equality were part of the community life . . . hers and theirs.

Most miraculous it seemed to Marian that her people had had a notable past! For in school she had read and learned only of Anglo-Saxon exploits and heroism. As a Jewess she had felt that she, like Topsy, "just growed." Actually, there was no preparation for life in idealistic Palestine, more fitting than the training given by the Ethical Culture Society, were it followed to its logical conclusion. What her parents and teachers had failed to realize, Marian felt, was that stress on ethical relationships between man and man, presupposes ground under man's feet. A position from which to adjust himself outward. For the first time in her life, here in Palestine she felt she met Jews on a common ground, their own Land.

To express her reactions to others was more difficult. She wrote to her family, "How we misjudged those Russian Jews at home! For here the builders of a new community and new culture are primarily Russians and Poles. Those awkward 'foreignisms,' dubbed as such by the melting-pot advocates of conformity, are lost here where the Jew is enveloped by a friendly Jewish environment. Here he is accepted on face value and plunges whole-heartedly into constructive labor. Jewish workers perform every task, be it lofty or menial, which is needed for Jewish living.

"In Palestine," she wrote, "there is for almost every one a strong releasing identification with the soil, and a psychic readjustment which takes into consideration the changing seasons and the shifting winds. Here is the happiness of those who, having lived in cities with books, and having known foreign cultures, and dwelled in many lands, are at least come together with their own kind. They are determined to live according to their own ethical and spiritual standards . . . to be Jews among Jews, and measured by their own inherent standards.

"Sometimes, when I wake early of a morning," she wrote, "and set myself in the right frame of mind for another Hebrew-speaking day, I wonder can this be the same I that I was."

GUIDE TO "MARIAN SANDERS' STORY"

1. How typical is this story of American Jews
   (a) In relation to home ceremonies—"Christian" atmosphere;
   (b) in relation to economic status and schooling:
   (c) in relation to parental objectives.
2. Notice how first awareness of being a Jew arises. Compare it with experience of Dr. Steinberger, Jessie Sampter.
   In the light of Lewin's theory how and when should a child acquire awareness of being a Jew?
3. What is the attitude toward a "foreign" language in general, in America?
   (a) In New York, a cosmopolitan center;
   (b) in "foreign" centers like German sections of Middle West, Chicago or San Francisco;
   (c) in strictly "American" circles.
   (d) How does this differ from the attitude toward Yiddish? How do you account for this in the light of Lewin's self-hatred theory?
   (e) Notice that the study of Hebrew is the first outward sign of a full return to their people on the part of Marian Sanders and Jessie Sampter. (See Aimee Paliere's book, "The Hidden Sanctuary." The reaction to Hebrew on the part of a convert to Judaism.)
4. Notice the need for some group affiliation on the part of every individual; many unaffiliated Jews turned to Ethical Culture.
   (a) Discuss Communism as another half-way group open to Jews who are adrift but seeking the sense of belongingness in some group; the necessity for obtaining a feeling of security in a group backed by a large, powerful, dominant country like Russia. Such affiliation gave great sense of security and importance to many escapist Jews.
5. Notice the joy which ceremonial gives in the celebration of Christmas, (in Sampter's case, too,) especially when the ceremonial is not that of the "inferior" group. Ceremonial is the poetry of the group; but Jewish ceremonies are rejected ostensibly on intellectual grounds—really a manifestation of self-hatred. By contrast see the joy, ease and freedom in the celebration of Purim and Passover in Eretz Yisrael.
6. In each case, Sampter and Sanders, there were emotional crises. Each felt insecure, unrooted. Sampter found that wholeness, escape from the periphery, in Zionism only after a series of religious experiences —Christian and Jewish; to Marian Sanders, Zion came whole, in a flash—full of sudden meaning. Both are experiences similar to reli-

gious conversion, but both of these Jews found full self-fulfillment in identification with a group to which they could belong fully, openly and with deep admiration. When self-hatred gave way to self-respect through respect for their people, poise and a sense of security was achieved.

(Re-read "The Island Within" where you can see something of the same psychological process in Arthur Levy.)

7. Felix Adler's appeal to save Marian from Zionism failed because his diagnosis was wrong. He substituted artificial groupings for the pulsating, natural ones of a historic people. Art, science, sport groupings, are necessary and enriching to life, but cannot substitute for the more fundamental people-group which gives us our fundamental outlook on life, the basic values by which we live.

8. The reaction to Eretz Yisrael is one of elation. Nature, the people, the social organization, everything in the land, conspired to produce the fullest meeting of the self with the group. This is true of Sampter too.

9. Released from the continuous awareness of belonging to a despised minority, the personality begins to flower. Marian Sanders feels that, freed from the necessity to engage her energies in negative anti-defamation type of activity, the Jew can, in Eretz Yisrael, divert his energies to positive creativity.

10. Discuss the possibility that identification with the cause of Zionism can release the fears and unhappiness of self-hatred, without settlement in the land. A phychological release from complexes follows on Zionism. Why?

    (a) Consult Lewin's theory again. Recognition of the normalcy and creativeness of the Jewish people is involved. See Namier point No. 7, Steps I and II in our outline. See also bottom of p. 72 in Marian Sander's story: "If only we could prove ourselves in Palestine, all Jews everywhere would know it can be done. We can live a free creative life wherever we are."

COLLATERAL READING

In order to familiarize yourself with the world of ideas and ideals of Pioneering Palestine, which influenced both Marian Sanders and Jessie Sampter so profoundly, the reader is referred to *Pioneer Youth in Palestine,* by Shlomo Bardin, Bloch Publishing Co., New York, 1932, particularly Chapters II and III.

A CONFESSION
by
Jessie Sampter

THIS HALF century which I have lived has changed human affairs so rapidly, has made so much history, that I am its faithful child in having also in my life traversed ages of experience. This, the half century of electricity, ushered out Queen Victoria, free competition, positivism and the horse-and-buggy, and ushered in the telephone, telegraph, cable, X-ray, automobile, airplane, cinema, radio, television, Russian Communism and Italian Fascism. I was born into a German-Jewish, third generation American upper middle class, well-to-do, completely assimilated, highly cultured bourgeois and individualistic family in New York City, where *trefe* meat was eaten as often as three times a day, where Christmas trees and Easter eggs obliterated all traces of *Hanukkah* and *Passover,* whose prophet was not Moses but Darwin. My maternal grandfather ate on *Yom Kippur* and my paternal grandmother made fun of people who kept *kosher.* I am now a citizen of Palestine, a vegetarian. I am a member of a Socialist-Zionist commune of agricultural and industrial but highly cultured workers, the chief aim of whose rapidly growing and penurious settlement is to bring as many Jews as possible, as quickly as possible, to our ancient home land. Having crossed continents, literally and figuratively, from one civilization to another, I know into the depths of my being what civilization means and what it does not mean. I know what are the eternally human and what are the transiently provincial things, what is international and what is national, what in me is human and what in me is Jewish.

In a godless household of Ethical Culturists, I got God from the servants by the time I was seven. I knew him quite intimately and prayed to him nightly to beg him to make a good girl of me. I also got from these same servant girls an ineradicable sense of human equality. But if they, or anyone, ever told me I was Jewish, it made no impression. When I was seven years old, some children in the street told me I was Jewish, which impressed me exactly as if they had told me I was a rag-picker, a gypsy or an idiot. I denied it hotly. I went home to be enlightened, to pass through the fire of indignation into a defender of my race, but to continue to hang up my Christmas stocking and to paint my Easter eggs.

When I was fifteen, having already tasted tragedy* and swallowed it down, the childish religion with which I tried to sugar-coat bitter reality split and broke under the pressure of maturing thought. I became an atheist, who had loved God and had lost him. Life was an empty and horrible void. I sought a way out. I sought above all to understand first the pain and grief of life, second, the absence of God who was supposed to have made this now meaningless and fatherless world. The world and I—we were both orphans; yet we were. It became necessary to explain not only death and pain but life and joy, thought, beauty and love. I remember, as a turning point, one night on the seashore realizing first the vast sea, then the stars—each star a sun larger than our sun, this earth a grain of dust and I, dust of dust—and suddenly realizing who was thinking this thought. It was I. This infinity which terrified me lived in my own mind. And terror became awe. I remember a woman's red hat flash among green trees in a park near Paris, and the instantaneous realization that beauty justifies life. My mind that day was a raw sore, and the flash of color was a balm, as of a loving healer's hand. To me that which replaced God, the God recreated in turmoil out of the night emptiness, the realization of Being as in the beginning out of the chaos of my own heart, could never become that symbol of fatherhood, of clanhood, of nationality and later of humanity to which the peoples prayed and pray. Such a God has his place in history; he is responsible for and created by civilizations and changes with them. He is a symbol like a flag, a concrete something which smaller minds need, in order to realize the unseen whole, a handle for the emotion to grasp and hold fast. His "Thou shalt" and "Thou shalt not," his morality, is the morality of the people or peoples he represents. My God refound was not

---

* At that age, a serious illness left her permanently crippled.

a moral God, though morality be a necessary part of that universe —or of that part of that universe called humanity—whose very existence proclaims him. My God was an inner experience, a Presence felt and understood but not to be expressed in prose, an overwhelming realization to be expressed incompletely but passionately in poetry, music, art and in the way of life itself. Half my life ago in crisis, terror, sacrifice and resurrection, I found the answer to the questions I had asked after my childish world crashed, and though the name may not have been well chose, I then called the answer God.

Today I do not care to use that name.

My God was neither Jewish nor Christian. He needed no congregation. Yet I found him reflected in humanity, in great art and literature, and therefore also in parts of both sections of the Bible. But my solitary heart needed a congregation. Personal life had failed me, left me empty yet over-rich with spent and unspent love. So I went to seek for a congregation and I found a Unitarian Church. The words of the minister and the psalms he said tallied with the words in which I might and did express what I felt. But the ways of this congregation did not tally with what I needed. This congregation was not mine. Their societies were polished surfaces. Their charity was not love. All their ways were comfortable, self-satisfied and superior. This people was not my people. Then, one Sunday, when I had almost left them, I heard read from this pulpit parts of a modern Jewish book. Suddenly, as I had seen myself in the stars, I saw myself in the Jewish people. This was my congregation, this scattered, persecuted, poverty-stricken and divided people. My people, my congregation. At that moment I passed over from one kind of life into another. My God had spoken.

My first step, then, into my heritage was not Zionism nor Judaism; it was the acceptance of the Jewish people as my congregation. Through what I knew of the Bible—and I then knew the Bible well in English—and through this one modern poem which I had heard, the "Book of Pain Struggle," by Hyman Segal, and no doubt at all also through something in my direct spiritual inheritance, I experienced the Jewish people as my people and as historically and inevitably engaged in seeking to understand and to do what life has predestined within man and what, for want of a clearer expression, I now called the will of God. At first I rejected Zionism. What could geography have to do with an inner struggle? Very soon, however, I saw the connection, the need for earth under our feet and the meaning of history to a people. Before this, being absorbed in biology, psychology and philosophy, history had meant nothing to me. I had been a theoretical, a "parlor Socialist," I could not find contact with the materialism of the Socialist party. Now I found my Socialism in Zionism which meant to me the resettlement of Palestine by the Jew—whose Prophets were to my mind the first Socialists—in the spirit of social and economic equality. I found that spirit among the Zionists of New York's East Side.

From the acceptance of Zionism, I passed quickly to my own interpretation of Judaism. In this I had three teachers, three who stand out from many. Henrietta Szold, in whose household I saw the grace and beauty of traditional forms and who initiated me into an understanding of the synagogue service which made it possible for me to find truth, goodness and beauty, that is, poetry, in the set prayers, and to penetrate the depths of feeling among a mixed and distracting group of worshippers; Dr. Mordecai Kaplan, who opened my eyes to the true place of the Bible in Jewish life, not as history, not as miracle, not as religion, but as the history of the unfoldment of the Jewish spirit. My third teacher was the Jewish people itself, as I found it on the East Side of New York City, where I went to live in order to be among my own. I learned Hebrew, and as I learned I had the distinct feeling that I was remembering something known long since and long forgotten. I entered into rich treasures of thought, old and new; and as I came to know my people better, I saw that those who had preserved these treasures and those who were creating new values for Jewish life in America and Palestine were embodying the traditional Jewish customs and ceremonies in their daily lives. I saw these customs ridiculed or neglected by those who were carried along by other customs just as rigid but different, unintegrated and mechanical. Hanukkah replacing Christmas, Passover Easter, and Saturday the Sunday Sabbath, gave meaning and distinction to the fact of my Jewishness. The sufferings of the Jews were as my sufferings, their weakness as mine, their power and overcomings and their future were mine. In the space of a few years I lived through intensively what I had missed for generations. In synagogue service, in diligent study and in traditional living among the poor of my people, I recapitulated my lost history.

Then I came to Palestine . . .

Judaism is the way of life of the Jewish people. A Jewish way requires Jewish ground under our feet and Jewish enterprise. It implies a past and a future, history and prophecy, memory and direction in the eternal present. We can have all these only in Palestine. Having all these in Palestine, the Jews everywhere can listen in and dance to our tune, if they like, or reinterpret our melodies which, after all, are best and sweetest when we have reinterpreted them from theirs. Judaism, frozen so long by exile, hate and oppression, must now become completely fluid. We must not be afraid to let it set in entirely new patterns which, let us hope, will now be the banks of living streams.

But the eternally wandering, home-loving Jew is both introvert and extrovert. That is our peculiar fate, to see both sides. That accounts for Moses and for Spinoza. It presages what I have believed these many years and believe today and cannot doubt: A new light is coming into the world, as it has always come in moments of darkness and must come as inevitably as the sun rises. "Eternity's sunrise." A new *Baal Shem Tov* or another Massiah. Not the last, nor the first. A new synthesis of our hate of war and love of our land, of our social reconstruction and our individual deepening, of radios and music, machines and art, time and eternity, man and God.

Not reconstruction, but rebirth. Or are these only different words for the same prophecy?

"Not by might and not by power, but by my spirit, saith the Lord."

Reprinted from *The Reconstructionist*, Vol. III, No. 4, with the permission of the editors.

GUIDE TO "JESSIE SAMPTER"

1. Notice the absence of a special Jewish quality in Jessie Sampter's home. No ceremonies, no religious life, no awareness of the Jewish people.
2. How had she first learned she was a Jew? Can such an unhappy first knowledge be conducive to mental health?
3. Notice the collapse of her individually-created, childish religion and outlook in the face of tragedy. No deep roots of human experience were there to steady her. She could not rely on the funded experience of her people to help her meet her own sorrow.
4. What was her first positive Jewish step? (Realization of Israel, *the people* as a fact, "The Acceptance of the Jewish People.")
5. How does she describe her second step—"the acceptance of Zionism?"
6. Notice how Zionism brings with it a complete harmony in her attitude to all of Judaism. Notice, too, that her chief teacher was the "Jewish people itself."

FROM THE DIARY OF DR. HISSIN

INTRODUCTION

OUR ADJUSTMENT problems seem so new, so contemporary to us, that it is startling to find a Jewish student writing in 1882 in Russia as if he were a child of the sad twenties and thirties of the 20th century. Dr. Hissin, the author, was one of those Jews who leaped at the opportunity opened up by the liberal Russification movement initiated in about 1856 under Alexander II, when Jews flocked to the Russian schools; opened their minds to the culture of Russia and layed their souls at her feet in an access of patriotism. Their rude awakening was occasioned by the regression in 1881 under Alexander III which saw the flood gates of hate, plunder, murder and pogrom, break again in all its fury on an unsuspecting people. All these political facts are mirrored in the psychological odessy of Hissin from assimilation to Zionism.

"I had never before worried about the question of my origin. I felt myself a devoted son of Russia. It was in her life I lived and breathed. Every discovery by a Russian scientist, every well-received work of Russian literature, every success of Russia as a power, filled my heart with pride. I intended to devote my strength and energy to serving the interests of my country, and to honestly fulfill the obligations of a good citizen ... And now suddenly we are shown the door and are told 'the western frontier is open to us!' One serious, ruthless question haunts me: 'Who are you?' Why, who am I? I try to evade the question by another question—Ought I necessarily to classify myself, to be someone?

But it is inescapable. I must commit myself. 'Of course I am a Russian,' I venture, and in the same breath accuse myself of insincerity. Upon what is such a reply based? Isn't it merely upon desires and dreams alone? Can't you see, self, all you receive from (this) country (of your adoption) for your devotion is cold contempt. Everywhere we are looked upon as strangers and are pushed aside or ousted. We are not members of her national family, but are aliens, newcomers. No!—first of all I am a Jew. But are the only bonds between me and my race our mutual persecutions, our sufferings? True we had a great past. We are the breeding grounds of culture. But our aims now—our purpose? What besides memories can Jewry offer me? With what purpose and spirit of group endeavor can I fill out my life? I shiver at the thought of the life that confronts me, a life full of stifled moral pain, of subjection to innumerable petty insults, of paralyzed action—a horrible prospect for a sensitive Jew."

A deeply-rooted psychological conflict with all its consequences is apparent from this diary. That conflict was unknown to the old conformist Jew, and was passed unnoticed by the greater number of Eastern European Jewry. It was a logical effect of assimilation. Thousands of Jewish youth in Europe and America are oppressed by this psychological embarrassment and doubt. Sooner or later for most of them the question takes form: Who am I, What relation do I bear to the country of my sojourn? Out of the midst of what national warmth do I function? Of what human organism am I an integral part? The conflict remains. Only perhaps by an orientation of themselves in regard to that vital pioneer undertaking and achievement of their people in Palestine may their haunting question be resolved into the peace of an adequate solution and a satisfactory answer.

The diary continues:

"Among us grew up a movement for the colonization of Palestine. I gave much thought to this question and came to the conclusion that this is the only possible way for our people. My doubts are dissipated. There is a great future ahead of the Jews: a grand historical mission. Jewry is still struggling on a wide front of endeavor that can and must utilize the energy and strength and abilities of her devoted sons. I found new content and meaning in the word 'Jew.' It is worth working for—this great idea of regeneration. But to give up the consummation of my studies, to take plow in hand in a strange wild country! I had spent so many years here in school, I had grown accustomed to looking forward to a scientific career.

And now—so near the goal—to leave it all—exchange it all for the hard labor of a farmer! It was a violent struggle within me. I seemed to be in the throes of a high fever, till I decided. Now I feel quiet, and balanced, and calm. I know now what I want..."

* Reprinted by Permission from "Pioneer Youth In Palestine."

QUESTIONS ON "DR. HISSIN"

1. Notice the desire even in Russia in 1882 to be part of the majority group.
2. What forms does the desire to escape take?
3. Notice the terrible disillusion that follows upon his eager desire for impossible assimilation.
4. How does he find himself? Why does work for Palestine even before it was a flourishing community give him such inner peace?

COLLATERAL READING

1. For Hissin: Note especially Chapter I in Shlomo Bardin's *Pioneer Youth in Palestine*, which gives the background and setting for early efforts at self-realization in Eretz Yisrael.
2. For Sampter: See the reference appended to the Guide to Marian Sanders.
3. See also Jessie Sampter's *A Confession*, in Vol. 3, No. 5, in The Reconstructionist, a companion article to the one we have used here.

LOUIS DEMBITZ BRANDEIS

By
Louis E. Levinthal

LONG before his death, Louis D. Brandeis had become a tradition both in American life and in the Zionist movement. About his name and personality there had accumulated a mystical aura. He stood in an historical perspective even while he was contemporary. The seclusion forced upon him by his membership in the Supreme Court stimulated the growth of legends and anecdotes about him. An unconscious tribute of this nature has in this instance mitigated the profound sorrow which inevitably followed on his death. Already in his lifetime he had been possessed by the ages.

The name of Brandeis is second to none in the list of those who have placed the impress of their genius on the development of American jurisprudence, particularly our constitutional law. His contributions to law, economics and social science will be long remembered by Americans generally; his services to the Jewish people will never be forgotten by American Jews, and especially by American Zionists. And even in the sphere of his specifically American activities, although his approach was "new" and "modern," his inspiration was derived from his spiritual ancestors, the Prophets of Israel, with their passion for justice and righteousness. For this reason it is difficult to dissociate the Jewishness of Mr. Justice Brandeis from his secular legal and judicial career. This memoir will seek to deal with his relationship to Jewish life and thought, but even such specialized treatment will be understood only when it is realized that his life as a whole knew no contradictions or conflicts, but was built on a definite single pattern of consistent ideas and ideals.

I

LOUIS D. BRANDEIS was born in Louisville, Kentucky, on November 13, 1856. Of his early years we know little except that he lived the normal boyhood of a child of a well-to-do family, and that the bitter struggle between slave and abolitionist sentiment in his native state preceding and during the Civil War made a deep and vivid impression upon his young mind. His education in a private school was supplemented by travel abroad and by a short period at a German academy, where his free spirit rebelled against the strict discipline of that institution.

In 1877 he was graduated from the Harvard Law School with an extraordinarily brilliant record, and began the private practice of law in St. Louis. Beckoned, however, by friends and associations in Boston, he soon returned to that city, where he lived for close to forty years until his appointment in 1916 to the bench of the Supreme Court of the United States.

He achieved professional distinction early. The law firm with which he was associated represented many large corporations, and his practice was highly lucrative. He did not permit this fact to influence his personal code, however, nor his evolving conception of justice and right. Thus, while his firm handled cases for life insurance companies, he campaigned against certain questionable practices of these concerns, and advocated the establishment of savings bank life insurance for the public benefit. While he was acting as the legal representative of railroads, he publicly attacked certain policies of one of the most powerful systems as inimical to the interests of the people. He resigned as attorney for the largest shoe machinery company in the country and attacked it as a monopoly. At his own expense he served as counsel to establish the validity of such progressive legislation as the statutes fixing maximum working hours for women and establishing minimum wages for employees. It was this active interest in the rights of the inarticulate common man, which he defended against highly organized predatory interests, that won him his popular title of "the people's attorney."

Indeed, it is rather remarkable that his social ideology and liberal outlook developed as they did. Prosperity came early to Louis D. Brandeis; he moved in the circles of his wealthy professional colleagues. He was secretary of the Boston Art Club and a member of a fashionable boat club; he was associated with a society polo group. That a man in this environment, and subject to these influences, should become a champion of the downtrodden, a pioneer of social security, an exponent of broad democracy, is evidence of unusual character.

It was not strange, therefore, that Woodrow Wilson's appointment of Brandeis, the first Jew to be named to sit on the bench of the United States Supreme Court, did not go unchallenged. All the reactionary elements which had been exposed or attacked by "the people's attorney," together with many misguided individuals, joined in the hue and cry to prevent his confirmation by the Senate. In replying to the opposition to Brandeis, President Wilson said: "He is a friend of all just men and a lover of the right; and he knows more than how to talk about the right — he knows how to set it forward in the face of its enemies."

After protracted and heated debate, Brandeis was seated in June, 1916. His judicial interpretations of the Constitution during his twenty-three years on the Supreme Court and his concept of the living and developing law have already made history. The basic principles which found expression in his legal and judicial career provide a key to his character and to an understanding of the consistent pattern of his interests and ideals. To him law was made to serve the people, not the people to serve the law. Neither was law drawn only from precedents. It was drawn from the living, breathing reality of men and women who sought to live together in peace and understanding. He was willing to strike out in uncharted fields to find adequate solutions. Dean James M. Landis of the Harvard Law School, in his memorial address before the Brandeis Lawyers Society of Philadelphia, said in this regard: "There is no better justification of the significance of the right of freedom of expression to the maintenance of a civilization that would base itself upon the rationality of mankind than his closing sentence in *New State Ice Co. vs. Liebman*: 'If we would guide by the light of reason, we must let our minds be bold.'"

As lawyer and as judge, Brandeis introduced the method of using scientific data furnished by the sociologist and economist, and sought to have the law keep step with the march of time as reflected in the living conditions of men and women. But many of his briefs and decisions were also based on the importance and value of human intangibles. In one of his notable opinions he wrote: "The makers of the Constitution undertook to secure conditions favorable to the pursuit of happiness. They recognized the significance of man's spiritual nature, of his feelings and of his intellect. They knew that only a part of the pain, pleasure and satisfaction of life are to be found in material things. They sought to protect Americans in their beliefs, their thoughts, their emotions and their sensations . . ."

II

THE story is told, whether factual or legendary, that shortly after President Wilson had appointed Brandeis to the Supreme Court, a friend said to the President: "Isn't it a pity, Mr. President, that a man as great as Mr. Justice Brandeis should be a Jew?" Instantly the President replied: "But he would not be Mr. Brandeis if he were not a Jew."

The causal connection between the Jewishness of Brandeis and his unique contributions to American law and jurisprudence is obvious. His passionate devotion to the welfare of the underprivileged and the dispossessed, of those who were denied that equality of opportunity which the founders of our Republic had intended all Americans to share; his yearning to make the life of the average individual, the little man, the forgotten man, more significant, more worth living; his battles, as lawyer and as judge, against economic tyranny in every form; his conviction that true democracy demands equal economic opportunity no less than equal political rights; his deep human sympathy; his gallant championship of American ideals of justice and righteousness — all these are identical with traditional Jewish ideals, which he derived from his Jewish background, from those common group memories and from that special aptitude in the field of social justice and ethics which he called "the Jewish heritage."

At first glance it would seem that Brandeis's acceptance of Zionism was a decision of the mind and not of the heart. There are some Jews who are brought to a realization of the Jewish problem by personal difficulties, large or small,—exclusion from a country club, discrimination in some more shocking form, or a violent contemporary outburst of anti-Semitism. Hurt, baffled, for the first time conscious of his insecurity, the individual seeks an answer. There was no such personal frustration in Brandeis's case. In every sense he felt personally secure; yet his keen, logical mind, when brought to bear upon the problem of the Jewish people, quickly grasped the basic elements of the question, and he was enabled to see beyond his own personal needs and desires. His mind grasped the significance of ancestral influences which his heart was prepared to receive.

His early Jewish education was scanty and his contact with the Jewish people remote; his accurate appraisal of the facts of Jewish life is therefore all the more remarkable. It might almost be said that in his first approach it was his instinct asserting itself—an instinct which was not wrong. That he believed there existed a "Jewish instinct" or an unconscious affiliation of the individual with his people, is revealed in one of his comments. "Let us not imagine that what we call our achievements are wholly or even largely our own," he said. "The phrase 'self-made man' is most misleading. We have power to mar, but we alone cannot make. The relatively large success achieved by Jews, wherever the door of opportunity was opened to them, is due, in the main, to this product of Jewish life, to this treasure which we have acquired by inheritance, and which we are in duty bound to transmit unimpaired, if not augmented, to coming generations."

Beneath the surface of his success as lawyer it was soon obvious that Brandeis was a product of Jewish life, and that the Jewishness of his ancestors operated through him. It is interesting to note that his maternal uncle, Lewis Naphtali Dembitz, a leading lawyer of Louisville, was a Jewish scholar of rare distinction, the writer of most of the articles on legal subjects in the *Jewish Encyclopedia,* and also the author of an authoritative volume on the synagogue service. Young Louis Brandeis must have been a great admirer of his uncle, for though his original name was Louis David, he early adopted the name of this favorite relative, and when he entered Harvard Law School it was as

Louis Dembitz Brandeis. And it should not be forgotten, to quote Emerson, that "every man is an omnibus on which all his ancestors are seated."

It is impossible to ascertain just when his Jewish consciousness began to manifest itself. His biographers relate that some time in the nineties, while in the west, he wrote his wife commenting favorably on the plan to rebuild Palestine. At any rate, not until 1910, when he was already 54 years old, is there available recorded evidence of his feelings on Jewish subjects. In a newspaper interview published on December 9, that year, Brandeis said of Zionism: "I have a great deal of sympathy for the movement and am deeply interested in the outcome of the propaganda. These so-called dreamers are entitled to the respect and appreciation of the entire Jewish people."

The same year, Brandeis first came into contact with the laboring masses of American Jewry and saw for himself their material poverty amid their potential spiritual richness. On the occasion of the New York garment workers' strike in that year, he served as the impartial chairman of the Arbitration Board, and he successfully negotiated a novel compromise plan which has been regarded as epoch-making in the development of American trade unionism. This intimate glimpse of his fellow-Jews among the employers and the employees in the garment industry made him at least an interested auditor when Jacob de Haas poured into Brandeis's ears the story of the Herzlian solution of the problem of the homelessness of the Jewish people. De Haas was one of the founders of Zionism in England, had known Theodore Herzl, had attended the first Zionist Congress at Basle, and was then the editor of an Anglo-Jewish publication in Boston.

There followed a period of absorbed study of the Zionist movement and its implications for Jewish life. He read everything within reach on the various aspects of the Jewish problem. Then, in March, 1913, came his first public participation in Zionist activities, when he served as chairman at a reception in Boston for Nahum Sokolow, one of the outstanding leaders of Zionism, who was then touring the United States for the cause. In the course of his brief remarks, Brandeis said: "The great message that Mr. Sokolow brought to Boston may sometime become a reality, and the Jewish people may establish the national state that they have aspired to and longed for so long. . . . The task ahead of them is to make this Zionist ideal a living fact."

It was after the outbreak of the World War in 1914 that the major responsibility for the continued existence of the Zionist movement had to be taken over by American Zionists. The Provisional Executive Committee for General Zionist Affairs was organized in August of that year, and Brandeis accepted the chairmanship of that Committee and the leadership of the movement. He took charge of Zionist administration, wrote a number of articles and addresses, and made a tour of a number of American Jewish communities in an effort to enlist their support for the Zionist cause.

Frequently, in these addresses, Brandeis pointed out that there are two aspects to the Jewish problem, that of the individual Jew and that of Jews collectively. He asserted on one occasion: "Jews collectively should likewise enjoy the same right and opportunity to live and develop as do other groups of people. This right of development on the part of the group is essential to the full enjoyment of rights by the individual." Seldom has there been so concise and so comprehensive a statement of the principle on which Zionism is based.

To Brandeis, Judaism was a way of life which should be preserved. "Death," he wrote, "is not a solution of the problem of life," and those who advocated assimilation, either by conscious pursuit of such a policy or by neglect of the Zionist-survivalist project, were actually un-Jewish. Zionism, according to Brandeis, aimed not only to rebuild the Jewish homeland in Palestine, but also to rebuild the Jewish people, to reconstruct Jewish life wherever Jews live.

He was especially interested in the work of those individuals who went to Palestine and assumed the personal burden of restoring the Homeland. The hardships which these pioneers endured were not in the nature of a misfortune; they were, rather, priceless character builders, he felt. These men were struggling toward an ideal of social perfection; they were evolving a cooperative commonwealth within which the individual citizen may best develop a creative, a self-respecting, a worthwhile personality. And he had "no fear of the Arab or of any other question," because he knew in his heart "that Jewish qualities are qualities that tell." Not long before he passed away he made a special contribution to Hadassah to establish playgrounds for the joint use of Moslem, Jewish and Christian children in the Holy Land. This was in accordance with his frequently expressed view that "prosperity for Palestine must mean prosperity for all classes of its inhabitants. No one who has been in Palestine can doubt that the Arabs have been greatly benefited by what the Jews have done there." In a letter to this writer, dated December 12, 1939, Brandeis wrote: "In the whole world, nothing finer, nothing nobler, is being achieved than by the young men and women in the agricultural settlements in Palestine."

Brandeis urged that the chief bulwark against spiritual and moral deterioration of the Jews of America is to develop in them, particularly in the educated Jews, the sense of *noblesse oblige,* a sense which could best be achieved through active participation in the Jewish renaissance through membership in the Zionist Organization. This conception of Zionism—far different from mere philanthropic pro-Palestinism—is all the more noteworthy in that it came from one who, as we have seen, had not been brought up in an intensely Jewish environment, and from one who had never been affiliated with that most ancient and most authentic of all living Jewish institutions, the Synagogue. Here was a demonstration that one could become a devoted Zionist by force of conviction, logic and reason, as well as through sentimental and emotional attachments and loyalties. And here too was another classic demonstration of the redeeming power of Zionism.

There was, of course, nothing new in his conception of Zionism. Others before him had given expression to the same ideas, both with regard to the solution of the Jewish problem, and with regard to the social ideals of Zion reborn. But the manner in which he found the answer provides a further illustration for the words he used in 1916, following an address by the Rev. William Blackstone at a Zionist convention:

"Those of you who have read with care the petition presented twenty-five years ago by the Rev. William Blackstone and others, asking that the President of the United States use his influence in the calling together of a Congress of the nations of the world to consider the Jewish problem, with a view to the giving of Palestine to the Jews, must have been struck with the extraordinary coincidence that the arguments which the Rev. Blackstone used in that petition were in large part the arguments which the great Herzl presented five years later in setting forth to the world the needs and the hopes of the Jewish people. That coincidence, the arguments presented in America, arguments later presented by Herzl without knowledge of the fact of what had been done in America, shows how clearly and strongly founded they are. They come to all men who will regard in a clear and statesmanlike way the problems of the Jewish people."

It has been frequently pointed out that Brandeis came to his Zionism via his Americanism. His faith in human freedom, his belief that the principles of the Declaration of Independence applied to all men and women and children everywhere, his passion for justice and righteousness, all these led him to espouse the cause of Zionism which was the application of these principles to the solution of the Jewish problem.

In fact, Brandeis saw in Zionism the means of realizing in Palestine more quickly and more completely those social ideals that America has striven, and is still striving, to make real. The advantage Palestine enjoys, he thought, is its relatively limited area. It is not too big for social and economic experimentation. Nor are there in Palestine powerful vested financial interests to impede industrial democracy and cooperative effort. He even conceived the very details of Palestine's upbuilding in American terms. The *Halutzim* (Jewish pioneers) were to him "our Jewish Pilgrim Fathers." And when he described the aridity of undeveloped Palestine, he referred to the experiences of the Puritans who upon landing at Plymouth met stony soil upon which they eventually founded a nation. And in the practical working out of Zionism, Brandeis urged that the movement be organized democratically and efficiently 'according to well-tried American methods.

He spoke of democracy on the American scene; he indicated the need for the same in the Jewish community. His sympathies were with the little people, the underprivileged and dispossessed, and who have been more often and more continuously dispossessed than the Jews? Brandeis attempted to apply the principle of democracy to Jewish life in America. He was chairman of the Jewish Congress Organization Committee which in 1916 led to the convening of the first American Jewish Congress in Philadelphia. He believed that there was need for a democratic body to express the will of the masses of American Jewry. In the field of relief work and in other matters affecting the Jewish people as a whole, he felt that the direction should come from the Jewish masses themselves. He was opposed to "secret diplomacy" or policies of evasion and indirection. "Secrecy," he wrote, "necessarily breeds suspicion, and creates misunderstanding."

It would not be fair to say that Brandeis created any new concept of Americanism, but undoubtedly he did define and clarify American democracy. He rejected the "melting pot" theory of Americanism, and advocated what has come to be known as "cultural pluralism" or "cultural democracy." The term he gave to what he regarded as the essential feature of true Americanism is "inclusive brotherhood." In his famous Fourth of July address, at Faneuil Hall, Boston, in 1915, he declared: "America, dedicated to liberty and the brotherhood of man, rejected the aristocratic principle of the superman as applied to peoples as it rejected that principle when applied to individuals... America has believed that in differentiation, not in uniformity, lies the path of progress.

"The movements of the last century have proved that whole peoples have individuality no less marked than that of the single person, that the individuality of a people is irrepressible, and that the misnamed internationalism which seeks the obliteration of nationalities or peoples is unobtainable. The new nationalism adopted by America proclaims that each race or people, like each individual, has the right and duty to develop, and that only through such differentiated development will high civilization be attained."

Brandeis further elaborated upon his concept of the distinction between nationhood and nationality in one of his most comprehensive statements on Zionism, entitled "The Jewish Problem—How to Solve It," where he wrote: "Likeness between members is the essence of nationality; but the members of a nation may be different. A nation may be composed of many nationalities, as some of the most successful nations are. An instance of this is... the American nation. The unity of a nationality is a fact of nature; the unification into a nation is largely the work of man. As a nation may develop though composed of many nationalities, so a nationality may develop though forming parts of several nations."

Thus he reached the conclusion that Zionism, far from being inconsistent with American patriotism, is actually, for the Jew in this country, the inevitable consequence of true Americanism.

"Multiple loyalties are objectionable only if they are inconsistent," he declared. "A man is a better citizen of the United States for being also a loyal citizen of his state, and of his city; for being loyal to his family, and to his profession or trade; for being loyal to his college or his lodge... Every American Jew who aids in advancing the Jewish settlement in Palestine, though he feels that neither he nor his descendants will ever live there, will be a better man and a better American for doing so."

These phrases have been quoted frequently, and yet it is still necessary to repeat them. Brandeis, too, realized the inability on the part of some Jews to think clearly on the subject, and he emphasized the fundamentals. "There is no inconsistency between loyalty to America and loyalty to Jewry," he said, and proceeded to indicate the positive affinity. "The Jewish spirit, the product of our religion and experiences, is essentially modern and essentially American. Not since the destruction of the Temple have the Jews, in spirit and in ideas, been so fully in harmony with the noblest aspirations of the country in which they lived." Zionism could not be divorced from this Jewish spirit because the two were identical.

Brandeis believed that Zionism was truly based on American ideals. To him, as to Thomas Jefferson and Abraham Lincoln, to Charles W. Eliot and John Dewey, the spirit of American democracy could best be nourished and our national achievements could best be enriched, if each nationality, each religious or cultural group, would develop to its utmost capacity, thus giving to American civilization its multiformed and multi-colored beauty and richness. He therefore declared: "Loyalty to America demands that each American Jew become a Zionist."

If the Zionist ideology of Brandeis was not novel, and if his conception of Americanism was not new, it was Brandeis's articulation of the synthesis of the two that will rank as his greatest contribution to American Jewish life.

From 1914 until his death, Brandeis's participation in Zionist work was whole-hearted and enthusiastic. Throughout the years of his service on the bench of the highest court of the land, he maintained a close and personal interest in the Zionist movement. Even after he withdrew from official leadership of the Zionist Organization of America in 1921, after an internal controversy between a group led by Dr. Chaim Weizmann, Dr. Shmaryahu Levin and Louis Lipsky, on the one side, and a group led by the Justice, Dr. Stephen S. Wise, Judge Julian W. Mack, Professor (now Mr. Justice) Felix Frankfurter, Jacob de Haas and Robert Szold, on the other, Brandeis never failed to renew his annual membership in the Organization. His financial contributions to Palestine, frequently anonymous, were munificent, and he bequeathed a considerable portion of his residuary estate to Jewish Palestine. But these pecuniary benefactions were, of course, relatively far less significant than his self-dedication to the cause of Zion's rebirth; and once having found "Zion," he never for a moment forgot it.

III

Louis D. Brandeis created no voluminous literature. We find occasional public testimony at hearings, magazine articles, legal briefs, addresses on Zionism, a few pamphlets, many letters, numerous judicial opinions, so often in the minority in those early years. These writings, limited in extent though they are, are rich in profound, incisive thought, clearly and compactly expressed.

His greatness is not to be found, however, in his utterances or writings. It was in the man himself, in his unique personality, that there were indefinably epitomized a school of thought which may be labelled "American" and also a philosophy of life which may be called "Jewish," and it was in his very being that these two—Americanism and Jewishness—were synthesized. And just as there are those who still lag behind his juristic, social and economic pioneering, there are also those who have not yet attained his acute perception of the essence of American democracy and of what he liked to call "the Jewish spirit."

He was simple and unassuming. He eschewed all ostentation. His home in Washington, his summer cottage in Chatham, on Cape Cod, were unpretentious, even austere. Lavishness and gaudiness, display and extravagance were hateful to his orderly mind. His humble surroundings were reflections of his character, for his personal manner, too, was reserved and unassuming. He was never reluctant to admit his own shortcomings, and when taking over leadership of the American Zionist movement, he declared publicly: "I feel my disqualification for this task. Throughout long years which represent my own life I have been to a great extent separated from Jews. I am very ignorant of things Jewish..."

His simplicity, however, never partook of asceticism; his reserved demeanor and impassive attitude were never cold or unsocial. Rather were they marks of the control and discipline which he exercised over himself. He had genuine warmth and a sparkling personality, as those who had occasion to meet with him frequently have reason to know. Visitors to the Brandeis household were always touched by the considerate and affectionate relationship which obtained between the Justice and his charming wife and companion (who before her marriage to Mr. Brandeis in 1891 was Alice Goldmark) and their two daughters. Included in his long and crowded daily schedule, beginning soon after sunrise, there was always time set aside for his grandchildren with whom he loved to play and discourse.

Genuinely, and in the full meaning of the word, he was a leader, in that he was far removed from the trivial, the shoddy, and the mean in Jewish life and affairs. He was ever direct in speech, appreciative of loyalty, and tolerant of differing views. Indeed, his role in American Zionism was not always calm. There were interests and views which he felt called upon to combat, and he had the courage of his convictions. But he was blessed with the ability to remain above the petty strife which appeared to consume many about him.

It has frequently been noted that Brandeis had a passion for facts and that he was meticulous about details. Above all he was ever a pragmatic realist. It was his grasp of realities which made him insist on improvement of health and sanitation conditions in Palestine as a prerequisite to nation-building. He knew that a nation could not be built on a malarial swamp, that the first step must be the eradication of endemic sicknesses. And so he was keenly interested in the medical organization of Hadassah.

For two thousand years there had been dreams and visions and hopes. This time the Jews must deal in substantial and material things. He thought in Herzlian terms and used Herzlian language, and all his plans had a Herzlian swing. There were some dreamers who were disappointed in him because he kept his feet on the ground, and because he failed to soar with them; they thought he was lacking in the sentiment or the spirit of Zionism. But for all his realism and pragmatism, there were spiritual qualities which likewise possessed him, though perhaps they defied definition. Many a man upon first meeting the Justice, felt that there was something hauntingly mystic about his eyes and his voice, that he saw things too deep for mere expression in words.

Many American Jews could not understand him, for here was a man who quoted the Bible, Ahad Ha-am, Herzl, who referred to Aaron Aaronsohn, Ben Yehudah, and who, on the other hand, quoted Seton-Watson, W. Allison Phillips, Carlyle. He was a synthesis of two worlds. All his life represented the achievement of syntheses, and the reduction of conflicts. Many found it difficult to reconcile social reform and capitalism in his career and in his beliefs. This was because he freed himself from the encrusted meanings of those terms; he did not allow his actions to be influenced by connotations of words which foster prejudices. He was an attorney for business, but not for the evils of big business. He was a champion of labor, but was opposed to a dictatorship of labor as much as to a dictatorship of high finance. He was interested in, and to the end of his life supported, Hashomer Hatzair, a left-wing Zionist group, while at the same time he helped found the Palestine Economic Corporation, and played an important role in the encouragement of the investment of private capital in Palestine. His stand was not inconsistent, because he saw these groups as different facets of the same country.

A liberal in the modern economic sense of the word, he was not a Marxist. He was a believer in the system of private enterprise, though he felt that there were evils in the system which had to be corrected. He was a meliorist with the obstinate idea that change, both in American life and in the Zionist movement, must be based upon a realistic appreciation of facts.

Americanism and Zionism were inextricably interwoven in the fabric of the life of Louis D. Brandeis—a life which to the end was true to its pattern.

In announcing the death of Justice Brandeis, which occurred on October 5, 1941, Chief Justice Harlan F. Stone made this brief, formal statement to the Supreme Court of the United States:

"Learned in the law, with wide experience in the practice of his profession, he brought to the service of the Court and of his country rare sagacity and wisdom, prophetic vision and an influence which derived power from the integrity of his character and his ardent attachment to the highest interests of the Court as the implement of government under a written constitution."

This great tribute may, in all humility, be freely adapted to the Jewish side of his life: Conscious of the problems of the Jewish people, he brought to the service of his fellow-Jews "rare sagacity and wisdom, prophetic vision and an influence which derived power from the integrity of his character and his ardent attachment" to the cause of the survival of his people as a free and normal group among the families of mankind.

Reprinted from *American Jewish Year Book*, Vol. 44, with permission of the Publishers, The Jewish Publication Society.

GUIDE TO "BRANDEIS"

1. What is his training and in what groups does he find himself professionally and socially up to the age of 54?

2. How did his first Jewish interests arise? (Through contact with the Jewish garment workers in a New York strike case, through hearing of Herzl's plan from Jacob de Haas, through his study of the Jewish problem and Jewish history after this initial stimulus).

3. On what basis did Zionism appeal to him? We must understand his view of all peoples and their rights first. He completely assumed, as an American, the right of every group, (as strong as the right of every individual) to express itself fully and thus to contribute to human progress. Brandeis felt that each people has the right, nay, the *duty* to live fully and freely and to pursue its own individuality. This he based on the Bill of Rights which guarantees the individual's freedom. For Brandeis' driving motive is the application of these rights to all sorts of individuals and especially to all sorts of groups. The Jewish people, therefore, he assumes, have full rights to freedom and happiness and the duty to pursue them.

4. How did the social creativeness and the idealism of the chalutzim influence Brandeis? Notice that, again as an American, he understood and admired the pioneer.

5. What were his chief contributions to Zionism? How are they determined by his Americanism?

    (a) His position flows from the political tradition of America. Brandeis is essentially an American and his contribution is thus *the* American contribution to Zionism. His terms are American. Name some.

    (b) What were the contributions of Brandeis to Zionism?

    (c) He emphasized and applied the concept of "cultural pluralism" to the Jewish position in America.

    1. What is "cultural pluralism?" How does it differ from "totalitarianism" or the "melting pot" theory? Why is it especially necessary and possible in America? (See p. 95).

    2. What is the difference between nation and nationality according to Brandeis? (See pages 95-96). How does this apply to the Jews in America?

6. Note that unlike Herzl, it was not anti-semitism that brought him to Zionism.
7. Why could Brandeis' approach to Zionism appear only in America? Could you visualize such a theory arising in Europe?
8. Note Brandeis' statement that "to be a Zionist is to be a better American."

COLLATERAL READING

By LOUIS D. BRANDEIS:
> *The Jewish Problem and How to Solve It.*
> *True Americanism.*
> *Brandeis on Zionism*, Z.O.A., 1942.

HORACE M. KALLEN:
> The National Being and the Jewish Community in *The American Jew*—Ed by Oscar I. Janowsky, N. Y., 1943.

THEODORE HERZL

By
ALEXANDER BEIN

Theodore Herzl—or, to give him his Hebrew names, Benyamin Ze-ev Herzl—was born on Wednesday, May 2, 1860, in the city of Budapest. His childhood impressions must have been happy ones. The relationship between his parents was one of deep love strengthened by mutual respect for the qualities each needed in the other.

Almost next door to his father's house rose the liberal-reform temple. To this house of worship the little boy went regularly with his father on Sabbath and Holy Days. At home, too, the essentials of the rutual were observed, with particular emphasis on the celebration of two festivals, Hanukkah and Passover, the feast of lights and the feast of the Exodus. One touching ceremony which Theodore learned in childhood remained with him in his adult years; before every important event and decision he sought the blessing of his parents.

Even stronger than these impressions, however, was the influence of his mother. Her education had been German through and through; there was not a day on which she did not slip into German literature, especially the classic.

The Jewish world, not alien to her, did not find expression through her; her conscious efforts were all directed toward implanting the German cultural heritage in her children. Of even deeper significance was her sympathetic attitude toward the pride which showed early in her son, and her skill in transferring to him her sense of form, of bearing, of tactfulness and of simple grace.

At about the age of twelve—so Herzl told Brainin—he read somewhere in a German book about the Messiah-King whom many Jews still awaited and who would come riding, like the poorest of the poor, on an ass. The history of the Exodus and the legend of the liberation by the King-Messiah ran together in the boy's mind, inspiring in him the theme of a wonderful story which he sought in vain to put into literary form.

A little while thereafter Herzl was visited by the following dream: "The King-Messiah came, a glorious and majestic old man, took me in his arms, and swept off with me on the wings of the wind. On one of the iridescent clouds we encountered the figure of Moses. The features were those familiar to me out of my childhood in the statue by Michelangelo. The Messiah called to Moses: It is for this child that I have prayed. But to me he said: Go, declare to the Jews that I shall come soon and perform great wonders and great deeds for my people and for the whole world."

It may be to this period (of his *Bar Mitzvah*) of reawakened Jewish sensitivity, of heightened responsiveness to the expectations of his elders, of resurgent interest in Jewish historical studies (according to the testimony of one uncle)—it may be to this period that the dream of a dedicated life belonged. It is almost certain, too, that for the great event of the *Bar Mitzvah* the old grandfather of Semlin came to Pest. About this time, again, Alkalai, that early, all-but-forgotten Zionist, passed through Vienna and Budapest on his final journey to Palestine. Whether or not each one of these circumstances had a direct effect on the boy, the whole complex surrounds his *Bar Mitzvah* with the suggestion of the mission of his life, and, certainly, occasion was given for the awakening in him of the feeling of dedication to a great enterprise.

The attention, energy and time which Herzl devoted to literature, at fifteen, his absorption in himself, his activity in the school literary society meant of course so much less given to his school work. He found no time at all for science subjects; Jewish questions likewise disappeared from his interests; he was completely absorbed by German literary culture. This is all the more astonishing when we reflect that anti-Semitism continued to increase steadily. As a grown man Herzl could recall that one of his teachers, in defining the word "heathen," had said, "such as idolators, Mohammedans and Jews." Whether it was this incident,—as the memory of the grown man always insisted—which enraged him beyond endurance, or the increasingly bad school reports, or both circumstances together, the fact remains that on February 4, 1875 Herzl left the Technical School.

At sixteen to eighteen in High School, he struggled to define the basic principles of various literary art forms in order that he might see more clearly what he himself wanted to say. He took an active and eager part in the work of the "German Self-Education Society" created by the students of his school. The Jewish world, whose inferior position always wounded his pride, and whose obstinate separatism seemed to him utterly meaningless, drifted further and further out of his mind.

At eighteen, after the sudden death of his only sister, the family moved to Vienna where Herzl entered the University as a law student. Herzl, who accounted himself a liberal and an Austrian patriot, plunged eagerly into the activities of a large student Cultural Association, attended its discussions and directed its literary evenings. He had occasion, there, to deride certain Jewish fellow members who in his view displayed an excessive eagerness in their loyalty to various movements.

This was the extent to which, in these days, he occupied himself with the Jewish question—at least externally. He concerned himself little or not at all with the official Jewish world which was seeking to submerge itself in the surrounding world. He seldom visited the synagogue. His impulses carried him beyond the old and out-lived sphere—as he considered it—which had no more significance for him; beyond the "invisible Ghetto" into a more sincere and more aesthetic world, as the hero of his drama, *The New Ghetto* was later to express it.

He was an omniverous reader. His extraordinary knowledge of books was evident in his conversation, for he liked to adorn his speech with quotations, which came readily to his memory. Herzl read Eugen Dühring's book *The Jewish Problem as a Problem of Race, Morals and Culture*—the first and most important effort to find a "scientific," philosophic, biologic and historical basis for the anti-Semitism which was sweeping through Europe in those days (1881). Dühring saw the Jewish question as a purely racial question, and for him the Jewish race was without any worth whatsoever. Those peoples which, out of a false sentiment of humanity, had permitted the Jews to live among them with equal and sometimes even with superior rights, had to be liberated from the harmful intruder, had to be de-Judaized.

The reading of this book must have had upon him the effect—approximately—of a blow between the eyes. The observation set down in his diary burn with indignation: "An infamous book . . . If Dühring, who unites so much undeniable intelligence with so much universality of knowledge, can write like this, what are we to expect from the ignorant masses?"

The passionate reaction to Dühring's book, breaking forth in every sentence written down by Herzl, shows us how deeply he had been moved, and how fearfully he had been shaken in his belief that the Jewish question was on the point of disappearing. We shall find echoes of this experience in the pages of the *Judenstaat*. For the time being, however, he shrank from the logical consequences of his reactions. Only his inner pride began to build itself up.

The more immediate reaction was undoubtedly a sharpened perception and evaluation of his fellow-members in the Fraternity. Herzl had joined and been active in a duelling Fraternity. Here, too, anti-Semitism was breaking through; student after student expressed himself favorably toward the Jew-baiting speeches of Schoenerer, who was making a special effort to win over the universities. In the Fraternity debates Herzl expressed himself sharply against any open or covert manifestation of such sympathy. But he was already known for the sharpness of his tongue and the individuality of his views. Thus he won to himself neither the few co-religionists who belonged to the Fraternity nor the mass of the Germanic students. "He did not feel at ease among his comrades, and was to almost all of them an alien element."

He had learned from newpaper reports that the Wagner Memorial meeting, in which his Fraternity had taken a part, had been transformed into an anti-Semitic demonstration. His Fraternity had, therefore, identified itself with a movement which he, as a believer in liberty, was bound to condemn, even if he had not been a Jew. "It is pretty clear that, handicapped as I am by my Semitism (the word was not yet known at the time of my entry), I would today refrain from seeking a membership which would, indeed, probably be refused me; it must also be clear to every decent person that under these circumstances I cannot wish to retain my membership." In this honorable fashion Herzl withdrew from the organization.

On July 30, 1884, Herzl was admitted to the bar in Vienna. His student days were over. A new era opened for him, with its challenge to prove whether or not there was something in him to establish and proclaim to the world. His youth was finished.

In August, he entered on his law practice in the service of the state and was soon transferred to the court of Salzburg. Though he may at that time have been so far from Judaism that only pride and a decent respect for the feelings of his parents stood between him and baptism, he could not help perceiving that as a Jew he would find the higher levels of the civil service hierarchy closed to him. On August 5, 1885, he withdrew from the service in order to seek fame and fortune as a writer.

Brimming with hope, he set out on a journey which was to be the introduction to his literary life. He visited Belgium and Holland and in Berlin he made valuable connections and became a regular contributor to several big newspapers. Thus the range of his connections and relationships widened from year to year, and when he travelled again it was an ever-widening audience that waited for his impressions and observations.

In a book of reprinted feuilletons of Herzl which appeared in the first years of his success as a journalist a total of seven or eight lines is devoted to Jews. His impressions of the Ghetto in Rome. "What a steaming in the air, what a street! Countless open doors and windows thronged with innumerable pallid and worn-out faces. The ghetto! With what base and persistent hatred these unfortunates have been persecuted for the sole crime of faithfulness to their religion. We've travelled a long way since those times: nowadays the Jew is despised only for having a crooked nose, or for being a plutocrat even when he happens to be a pauper." Pity and bitterness inform these lines, but they are written by a detached spectator. He did not know how much of the Jew there was in him even in this detachment of his, in this feeling of remoteness from a world which offered him not living reality but folly.

In 1889 Herzl married; but the marriage was not a happy one. By 1892, Herzl had achieved great success as a dramatist and as a journalist; his plays had been performed on the stage of the leading theatre of Vienna and, to cap the climax came an oppointment to the staff of the *Neue Freie Presse,* one of the most distinguished papers on the continent.

Early in October he received a telegram from the *Neue Freie Presse* asking whether he would accept the post of Paris correspondent. He replied at once in the affirmative, and without even returning home, proceeded to the French capital at the end of the same month. He wrote to his parents: "The position of Paris correspondent is the springboard to great things, and I shall achieve them, to your great joy, my dear beloved parents."

Herzl sustained successfully the comparison with his great models and predecessors. In style as well as in substance his reports and articles were masterpieces of their kind. He came to his task with the equipment of a perfect feuilletonist; his style was polished and musical; he possessed in an exceptional degree the capacity to describe natural scenery in a few fine clear strokes and of hinting at, rather than of reproducing, a mood with a minimum of language. Everything was there, background, mood and development of action in plastic balance. It was only now, when a great opportunity provoked him to the highest effort, that all the lessons of the years of his apprenticeship built up a many-sided perfection.

He threw himself seriously and diligently into the journalistic craft. He observed with close attention all that went on about him, and listened with sharpened ears. But the moment had not yet come for the unveiling of a mission within him. Only, he was on the way; the process of preparation had begun.

How, in this mood of his, could he possibly have avoided clashing with the Jewish question? As far back as the time of his Spanish journey, when he had sought healing from his domestic and spiritual torments, the question had presented itself to him and had cried for artistic expression. His call to Paris had been a welcome pretext, perhaps, putting off the writing of his Jewish novel—the more so as he probably was not ripe enough for such an undertaking. Now that he was in Paris, where his eyes were opened to the full range of the social process, he began to draw nearer in spirit to his fellow-Jews, and to look upon them more warmly and with less inhibition. True, he found them as difficult aesthetically as before, but he tried hard to grasp the essence of their character and substance, and to judge them without prejudice.

When Herzl arrived in Paris this political tendency, anti-Semitism, had not—in spite of Drumont's exertions, and in spite of his paper, *la Libre Parole,* founded in 1892—achieved the dimensions of a genuine movement, nor was it destined to become one in the German sense. But it served as the focus for all kinds of discontents and resentments; it attracted certain serious critical spirits, too; its influence grew from day to day, and the position of the Jews became increasingly uncomfortable. It was ultimately to produce a crisis in the life of French Jewry not less than in the life of the French Republic.

Herzl's contact with anti-Semitism dated back to his student days, when it had first taken on the form of a social political movement. He had been aware of it as a writer, though the contact had never ripened into a serious inner struggle or compelled him to give utterance to it. As we have seen, he had already made the acquaintance of one of the basic books of modern anti-Semitism, and had reacted with passionate violence.

Now he read Drumont, as he had read Dühring. The impression was again a profound one. What moved him most in the work was the totality of a world picture based on a considered hostility to the Jews.

A ritual-murder trial was in progress in the town of Xanten, in the Rhineland. On August 31, 1892, Herzl, dealing with this subject as with all other subjects of public interest, summed up the general situation in a long report entitled "French anti-Semitism."

By now Herzl is no longer content with a simple acceptance of the facts; he is looking for the deeper significance of the universal enmity directed against the Jews. For the Jews this enmity is a hard school. For the world it is a lightning conductor. But he does not drive his inquiry further; so far it is only a flash of insight which ends in nothing more than a literary paradox. However, from now on it gives him no peace.

At the turn of the year 1892-93 there came a sharp clarification in his ideas, recorded in documents made public after his death. He had followed closely the evasive debates in the Austrian Reichstag—debates which forever dodged the reality by turning the question into one of religion. "It is no longer—and it has not been for a long time—a theological matter. It has nothing whatsoever to do with religion and conscience," declared Herzl brutally. "What is more, everyone knows it. The Jewish question"—he has reached a clear formulation—"is neither nationalistic nor religious. It is a social question."

Then came the summer, 1894, and at its close Herzl took a much needed vacation. He spent the month of September in Baden, near Vienna, in the company of his fellow-feuilletonist on the *Neue Freie Presse,* Ludwig Speidel. They went for long walks in the green meadows and philosophized at each other—landing, inevitably, in the midst of the Jewish question. Herzl has left a record of conversations. What he gave Speidel was more or less what he had felt, many years before, after his reading of Dühring. He admitted the substance of the anti-Semitic accusation which linked the Jew with money; he defended the Jew as the victim of a long historic process for which the Jew was not responsible. "It is not our fault, not the fault of the Jews, that we find ourselves forced into the role of alien bodies in the midst of various nations. The ghetto, which was not of our making, bred into us certain anti-social qualities . . . Our original character cannot have been other than magnificent and proud; we were men who knew how to face war and how to defend the state; had we not started out with such gifts, how could we have survived two thousand years of unrelenting persecution?"

For the time being Herzl was stuck half way along the road of discovery. He came across the Zionist solution, and definitely rejected it. Discussing the novel *Femme de Claude,* by Dumas the younger, he says of one of its characters: "The good Jew Daniel wants to rediscover the homeland of his race and gather his scattered brothers into it. But a man like Daniel would surely know that the historic homeland of the Jews no longer has any value for them. It is childish to go in search of the geographic location of this homeland. And if the Jews really 'returned home' one day, they would discover on the next that they do not belong together. For centuries they have been rooted in diverse nationalisms; they differ from each other, group by group; the only thing they have in common is the pressure which holds them together. All humiliated peoples have Jewish characteristics, and as soon as the pressure is removed they react like liberated men."

The inner apotheosis was drawing nearer and nearer for Herzl. Its footsteps rang ever louder in his spirit. In October, 1894, they sounded on the threshold. On the nineteenth day of that month Herzl was in the studio of the sculptor, Samuel Friedrich Beer, who was making a bust of him. The conversation turned to the Jewish question and to the growth of the anti-Semitic movement in Vienna, the hometown of both Herzl and Beer. It was useless for the Jew to turn artist and to dissociate himself from money, said Herzl. "The blot sticks. We can't break away from the ghetto." A great excitement seized Herzl, and he left the atelier, and on the way home the inspiration came on him like a hammerblow. What was it? The complete outline of a play, "like a block of basalt."

With this play—by far the best of his dramatic creations—Herzl completed his inner return to his people. Until then, with all his emotional involvement in the question, he had stood outside it as the observer, the student, the clarifier, or even the defender. He had provided the world-historic background for the problem, he had diagnosed it and given the prognosis for the future. Now he was immersed in it and identified with it.

He has become its spokesman and attorney, as he is spokesman and attorney for other victims of injustice. It is no accident that the hero of the play is a lawyer by vocation and avocation. For the hero is Herzl himself, and the transformation which unfolds in Dr. Jacob Samuel is the transformation which in unfolding in Theodore Herzl.

He belongs utterly to the Jews; it is for them that he fights, and, dying, he still sees himself as the fighter for their future. What future Jacob Samuel foresaw for the Jews in his dying moments remains unclear. It would appear that Herzl himself still believed that a deepening of mutual understanding between Jews and non-Jews might bring the solution.

But Herzl had travelled so much further by this time that he could not have in mind the "reconciliation" which would come by the capitulation of baptism. Indeed, the play emphasizes as a first prerequisite in human relations the element of self-respect. "If you become untrue to yourself," says the clever mother to the son, in the play, "you mustn't complain if others become untrue to you." It was like a fresh wind blowing suddenly through the choking atmosphere of a lightless room. It was a new attitude: decent pride!

It called for a frightful effort to descend from the intoxicating heights of creativity to the ordinary round of work. For weeks now his regular employment had filled Herzl with revulsion. The first reports of the Dreyfus trial, which appeared while he was working on his *New Ghetto,* therefore made no particular impression on him. It looked like a sordid espionage affair in which a foreign power—before long it was revealed that the foreign power was Germany, acting through Major von Schwartzkoppen—had been buying up through its agent secret documents of the French general staff. An officer by the name of Alfred Dreyfus was named as the culprit, and no one had reason to doubt that he was guilty, even though Drumont's *Libre Parole* was exploiting the fact of the man's Jewishness.

But, after the degradation of Dreyfus, Herzl was becoming more and more convinced of his innocence. "A Jew who, as an officer on the general staff, has before him an honorable career, cannot commit such a crime . . . The Jews, who have so long been condemned to a state of civic dishonor, have, as a result, developed an almost pathological hunger for honor, and a Jewish officer is in this respect specifically Jewish."

"The Dreyfus case," he write in 1899, "embodies more than a judicial error; it embodies the desire of the vast majority of the French to condemn a Jew, and to condemn all Jews in this one Jew. Death to the Jews! howled the mob, as the decorations were being ripped from the captain's coat . . . Where? In France. In republican, modern, civilized France, a hundred years after the Declaration of the Rights of Man. The French people, or at any rate the greater part of the French people, does not want to extend the rights of man to Jews. The edict of the great Revolution had been revoked."

Illumined thus in retrospect, the "curious excitement" which gripped Herzl on that occasion takes on a special significance. "Until that time most of us believed that the solution of the Jewish question was to be patiently waited for as part of the general development of mankind. But when a people which in every other respect is so progressive and so highly civilized can take such a turn, what are we to expect from other peoples, which have not even attained the level which France attained a hundred years ago?"

In that fateful moment, when he heard the howling of the mob outside the gates of the *École Militaire,* the realization flashed upon Herzl that Jew-hatred was deep-rooted in the heart of the people—so deep, indeed, that it was impossible to hope for its disappearance within a measurable period of time. Precisely because he was so sensitive to his honor as a Jew, precisely because he had proclaimed, in the *New Ghetto,* the ideal of human reconciliation, and had taken the ultimate decision to stand by his Jewishness, the ghastly spectacle of that winter morning must have shaken him to the depths of his being. It was as if the ground had been cut away from under his feet. In this sense Herzl could say later that the Dreyfus affair had made him a Zionist.

He saw all about him the ever fiercer light of a blazing anti-Semitism. In the French Chamber of Deputies the deputy Denis made an interpellation on the influence of the Jews in the political administration of the country. In Vienna a Jewish member of the Reichstag rose to speak and was howled down. On April 2, 1895, were held the municipal elections of Vienna, and there was an enormous increase in the number of anti-Semitic aldermen. Changing plans passed tumultuously through his mind. He wanted to write a book on "The Condition of the Jews," consisting of reports on all the important Jewish colonization enterprises in Russia, Galicia, Hungary, Bohemia, the Orient, and those more recently founded in Palestine, about which he had heard from his relative Löbl on his brief visit to Vienna. Alphonse Daudet, the famous French author with whom he had discussed the whole matter, felt that Herzl ought to write a novel; it would carry further than a play. "Look at *Uncle Tom's Cabin."*

He returned to his former plan of a Jewish novel which he had abandoned when he was called to his assignment on the *Neue Freie Presse* in Paris. Friend Kana, the suicide, was no longer to be the central figure. He was instead to be "the weaker one, the beloved friend of the hero," and would take his own life after a series of misfortunes, while the Promised Land was being discovered or rather founded. When the hero aboard the ship which was taking him to the Promised Land would receive the moving farewell letter of his friend, his first reaction after his horror would be one of rage: "Idiot! Fool! Miserable hopeless weakling! A life lost which belonged to us!"

We can see the Zionist idea arising. Its outlines are still indefinite, but the decisive idea is clearly visible; only by migration can this upright human type be given its chance to emerge. In *The New Ghetto* Jacob Samuel is a hero because he knows how to choose an honorable death. Now the death of a useful man is criminally wasteful. For there are great tasks to be undertaken. Life! Life is needed!

In essence it is the Act and not the Word that confronts us. What last impulse it was that actually carried Herzl from the Word to the Act it will be difficult to tell—he himself could not have given the answer. Little things may play a dramatic role not less effectively than great ones when a man is so charged with purpose as Herzl then was.

It is possible that something apparently irrelevant was the immediate efficient cause. On April 29, Herzl reported in great detail a catastrophe which has occurred near Epinal: a dam had collapsed, a great flood had burst over the countryside and more than a hundred human beings had been swept to their deaths.

This incident, coming at this moment, may have served as the liberating symbol for his own life. In him, too, a dam collapsed. In him, too, great floods were released to carry him away.

In the early days of May, Herzl addressed to Baron de Hirsch the letter which opens his Jewish political career. His request for an interview was granted. Herzl prepared an outline of his position in notes, lest he omit something important during their conversation.

In these notes he writes: "If the Jews are to be transformed into men of character in a reasonable period of time, say ten or twenty years, or even forty—the interval needed by Moses—it cannot be done without migration. Who is going to decide whether conditions are bad enough today to warrant our migration? And whether the situation is hopeless? The Congress which you (i.e. Hirsch) have convened for the first of August in a hotel in Switzerland. You will preside over this Congress of notables. Your call will be heard and answered in every part of the world.

"And what will be the message given to the men assembled? 'You are pariahs! You must forever tremble at the thought that you are about to be deprived of your rights and stripped of your possessions. You will be insulted when you walk in the street. If you are poor, you suffer doubly. If you are rich, you must conceal the fact. You are not admitted to any honorable calling, and if you deal in money you are made the special focus of contempt . . . The situation will not change for the better, but rather for the worse . . . There is only way out: into the Promised Land.'"

Where the Promised Land was to be located, how it was to be acquired, is not yet mentioned. Herzl does not seem to have thought this question of decisive significance; it was a scientific matter, as he later intimated. It was the organization of the migration which held his attention, the political preparations among the Powers, the preliminary changes to be brought about among the masses by training, by "tremendous propaganda, the popularization of the idea through newspapers, books, pamphlets, lectures, pictures, songs."

On the day of his conversation with Hirsch, Herzl wrote him a long letter in which he sought to supplement the information and impressions which had been the result of the meeting. "Please believe me, the political life of an entire people—particularly when that people is scattered throughout the entire world—can be set in motion only with imponderables floating high in the air. Do you know what the German Reich sprang from? From dreams, songs, fantasies, and gold-black bands worn by students. And that in a brief period of time.

"What? You do not understand imponderables? And what is religion? Bethink yourself what the Jews have endured for two thousand years for the sake of this fantasy . . .

"Certainly this national fantasy must rest on practical foundations. But whence have you the impression that I have no practical ideas for the details?

"But then I should have had to speak to you finally about the flag which had to be unrolled and under which the movement was to march. And then you would have asked me mockingly: 'A flag—what is that? A stick with a rag at the end of it.' No, *Monsieur le Baron,* a flag is a great deal more. It is with a flag that people are led whithersoever one desires, even to the Promised Land. For a flag men live and die; indeed, it is the only thing for which they are prepared to die in masses if they have been brought up to it.

"The exodus to the promised land presents itself as a tremendous enterprise in transportation, unparalleled in the modern world. What, transportation? It is a complex of all human enterprises which we shall fit into each other like cog-wheels. And in the very first stages of the enterprise we shall find employment for the ambitious younger masses of our people: all the engineers, architects, technologists, chemists, doctors, and lawyers, those who have emerged in the last thirty years from the ghetto and who have been moved by the faith that they can win their bread and a little honor outside the framework of our Jewish business futilities. Today they must be filled with despair, they constitute the foundation of a frightful over-educated proletariat. But it is to these that all my love belongs, and I am just as set on increasing their number as you are set on diminishing it. It is in them that I perceive the latent power of the Jewish people. In brief, my kind.

"In this letter of June 3, 1895, Herzl for the first time imparted his new Jewish policy to a stranger. The writing down of his views, as well as his conversation on the subject, had had a stronger effect on himself than on Hirsch. He had obtained a clear vision of the new and revolutionary character of his proposals. On the same day or shortly thereafter he began a diary under the title of *The Jewish Question.*

"For some time now, I have been engaged upon a work of indescribable greatness. I do not know yet whether I shall carry it through. It has assumed the aspect of some mighty dream. But days and weeks have passed since it has filled me utterly, it has overflown into my unconscious self, it accompanies me wherever I go, it broods above all my commonplace conversation, it peeps over my shoulder at the comical little journalistic work which I must carry out. It disturbs and intoxicates me."

Then suddenly the storm breaks upon him. The clouds open, the thunder rolls and the lightning flashes about him. A thousand impressions beat upon him simultaneously, a gigantic vision. He cannot think, he cannot act, he can only write; breathless, unreflecting, unable to control himself, unable to exercise the critical faculty lest he dam the eruption, he dashes down his thoughts on scraps of paper—"Walking, standing, lying down, in the street, at table, in the night," as if under unceasing command.

And then doubts rise up from the depths. He dines with well-to-do, educated, oppressed people who confront the question of anti-Semitism in a state of complete helplessness: "They do not suspect it, but they are ghetto-natures, quiet, decent, timid. That is what most of us are. Will they understand the call to freedom and to manhood? When I left them my spirits were very low. Again, my plan appeared to me to be crazy." Then at once he comes to "Today I am again as firm as steel," he notes the next morning. "The flabbiness of the people I met yesterday gives me all the more ground for action."

Clearer and clearer becomes the picture which he has of himself and of his task in the history of his people. "I picked up once again the torn thread of the tradition of our people. I lead it into the Promised Land."

"The Promised Land, where we can have hooked noses, black or red beards, and bow legs, without being despised for it. Where we can live at last as free men on our own soil, and where we can die peacefully in our own fatherland. Where we can expect the award of honor for great deeds. So that the offensive cry of 'Jew!' may become an honorable appellation, like German, Englishman, Frenchman—in brief, like all civilized peoples. So that we may be able to form our state to educate our people for the tasks which at present still lie beyond our vision. For surely God would not have kept us alive so long if there were not assigned to us a specific role in the history of mankind." He adds: "The Jewish state is a world need." He draws the logical consequence for himself: "I believe that for me life has ended and world history begun."

He let the first storm pass over him, yielding to its imperious will, making no effort to stem its fury, lest he interrupt the inspiration. When it had had its way with him, he took hold of himself again, and gathered up his energies for the effort to reconstruct everything logically and in ordered fashion. He was afraid that death might come upon him before he had succeeded in reducing to transferable form his historic vision. Thus, in the course of five days, he added to his diary a sixty-five page pamphlet—in effect the outline of *Der Judenstaat*—which he called: *Address to the Rothschilds.*

In the address he writes, "I have the solution to the Jewish question. I know it sounds mad; and at the beginning I shall be called mad more than once—until the truth of what I am saying is recognized in all its shattering force."

From a letter to Arthur Schnitzler. "These have been weeks of tremendous creative excitement, and I have sometimes feared that I was going out of my mind. For what moves me to believe that I have brought forth something of value is the fact that not for one instant have I been occupied with myself as the litterateur; I have been occupied solely with the great sufferings of others. A few days' work more, and the thing is completed in such wise that it cannot be lost, even though I should be prevented from carrying out the minutiae . . . You remember that dear poem of von Heyse's, 'To the Poet!'

> 'Longing, he might have died in the night,
> Ere the full work was brought to light.'

"That is my mood. I have deposited the material created till now in the Comptoir d'Escompte, strong box No. 6, shelf No. 2. The combination is: turn each of the three knobs seven times to the right. Someone must know this, lest 'I die in the night.' You are that one. Do I seem to you to be excited? I am not. I was never in higher or happier mood. I am not thinking of death, but of a life full of manly action, in which everything base, wild and corrupt that has ever been within me shall be extinguished, transformed and uplifted, and in which there shall be utter reconciliation between me and all men, through my work."

He wrote to Bismarck asking for an interview in order to submit his plan for a solution to the Jewish problem but he received no reply.

Now, in furtherance of his plan, he wrote on July 15 to Rabbi Gudemann, Chief Rabbi of Vienna, the occasion being the anti-Jewish excesses which had occurred in Vienna. "This plan . . . is a reserve against more evil days." Thus the interchange of letters with the Chief Rabbi of Vienna was resumed. "These wretched or cowardly men—or perhaps it is their wealth which has undone them—are enough to make one give up the work in disgust; but we must think, all the same, of the poor and decent Jews. They are the majority. We are not a chosen, but neither are we an ignominious people. That is why I am standing firm."

"There is for my plan a natural driving force. What is that force? The Jewish tragedy, the crying need of the Jewish people. Who dares to deny that this force exists?" Only now had Herzl discovered the practical foundation for his plan.

Herzl, in his first visit to England met and talked with Zangwill, whom he impressed without quite winning him over. But Zangwill made it possible for him to meet more than a few prominent, influential Jews of whom he made immediate converts. None of them wanted to know anything about the Argentine, and on this point the practical men were united with the dreamers: Palestine alone came into the picture for a national concentration of the Jews.

After his experiences in England, Herzl resolved to present his plan to the public at large. The *Address to the Rothschilds* which was the first complete writing of his plan, forged in the heat of inspiration was thoroughly reworked and emerged as his great book *Der Judenstaat*. Its title was: *The Jewish State: An Attempt at a Modern Solution of the Jewish Problem. Der Judenstaat* may properly be called Herzl's life work. His philosophy of the world, his views on the state, on the Jewish people, on science and technology, as we have seen them developing to this, his thirty-fifth year are concentrated in the book. What masterly clarity, what power and freshness, what proud self-certainty rings from the introduction! The sentences are like trumpet peals.

"The Jewish question exists. It would be stupid to deny it. It *is* a hangover of the Middle Ages, of which the modern civilized nations, with the best will in the world, cannot rid themselves. They showed their magnanimity when they emancipated us. The Jewish question exists wheresoever Jews are to be found in larger numbers. Where it does not exist it is brought in by immigrating Jews. We move naturally toward those areas where we are not persecuted; our appearance in those areas is followed by persecution. This is true, and it must remain true, even in highly developed countries—France proves it—as long as the Jewish question is not solved politically. The poorer Jews are bringing anti-Semitism into England; they have already brought it into America.

"I believe I understand anti-Semitism, which is an extremely complicated movement. I examine this movement as a Jew, without hate and without fear. I believe I recognize in it those elements which are merely brutal humor, mean stomach-envy, inherited prejudice, religious intolerance; but I also recognize the element of unconscious self-protection. I consider the Jewish question to be neither social nor religions, even though it takes on these and other colorations. It is a national question, and in order to solve it we must, before everything else, transform it into a political world question, to be answered in the council of the civilized peoples.

"We are *a people,* a people. Everywhere we have tried honestly to disappear in the surrounding community, and to retain only the faith of our fathers. We are not permitted to do it. In vain do we show our loyalty, and in some places an exaggerated patriotism; in vain do we bring the same sacrifices of blood and gold as our fellow-citizens; in vain do we exert ourselves to increase the glory of our fatherlands by achievements in art and science, the wealth of our fatherlands by our contributions to commerce. In our fatherlands, some of which we have lived in for many centuries, we are denounced as strangers: often by those whose forefathers were not yet in the land when ours were already sighing there. It is the majority which decides who is the stranger in the land: it is a question of power, as in all national relations . . ." Even when the Jews made the attempt to give up their existence as a people, the same enmity always flung them back upon themselves as an "historic group of recognizable interrelationship," i.e., as a people*. "He who is able to go under, he who must and wants to go under, let him do so. But the folk personality of the Jewish people cannot, must not and does not want to go under. It can not because external enmity keeps it together. It does not want to—this it had demonstrated in two thousand years of frightful suffering. It must not: that is what I attempt to establish with this book, following in the footsteps of many Jews who have not given up hope. Whole branches of the Jewish people can perish! the tree lives."

Thus, if no radical rescue is organized, the Jews must remain in a definite condition of distress wherever they live in larger numbers. The equality of rights guaranteed them by the law is abrogated in actual effect. "The simple fact is that everywhere the pressure issues to the same effect, and it is summed up in the classic Berlin cry: *Juden raus!* I shall therefore compress the Jewish problem into its capsule form: Must the Jews 'get out?' If so, whither? Or can we remain? And if so, for how long?"

The Jewish problem is to be solved by an exodus, by the gathering together of the people out of its dispersion, by its concentration in a land of its own, under its own government, responsible to itself; in brief, by the founding of the Jewish state. Political principle will provide the basis, technology will provide the means, the driving force of the great machine will be the Jewish tragedy, the guiding idea will be the Jewish state.

There is to be a complete break with the principle of "gradual infiltration of the Jews," such as has been accepted in the case of The Argentine and Palestine. For if immigration were attempted without this condition precedent of legal recognition, there would result the regular recurrence of an old phenomenon: "the government, under pressure of the local population, which would feel itself threatened by the immigration, would forbid the further influx of Jews. Emigration can therefore have sense only when it has as its foundation our assured sovereignty of the territory."

---

* Herzl rejected the race theory. "He accepts the racial point of view," he remarked regarding Zangwill, after their first meeting. "I have only to look at myself and at him in order to reject it. What I mean is: we are an historic unity with anthropological variations . . . No nation has uniformity of race."

"Let the word be repeated here which was given at the beginning: The Jews who will it shall have their state. We shall at last live as free men on our own soil and die peacefully in our own homeland. The world will be liberated by our liberation, enriched with our wealth, made greater by our greatness. And that which we seek there for our own use will stream out mightily and beneficently upon all mankind."

Condensed from Chapter I—VII, with permission of the publishers, The Jewish Publication Society.

GUIDE TO "THEODORE HERZL"

1. Here is the outstanding example of a great personality goaded into clear affiliation with his own group largely by anti-Semitism.

2. How much Jewish influence was there in his childhood? Was he concerned with Jewish questions in his youth and university days?

3. Notice the long period of literary creativity when Herzl was accepted as an important journalist and playwright in all of literary Europe. He seemed to have no great concern with Jewish issues at that time and suffered almost no personal effects of anti-Semitism.

4. Consider the influence on Herzl of his reading of Dühring's anti-Semitic book.

5. Note that Herzl at first thought Dreyfus guilty too, but the hatred of the mob, expressed in their triumphant joy at the suffering of a Jew, Dreyfus, confirmed Herzl in the conviction that no palliatory measures would help the Jew. If it could happen in enlightened France, he felt nothing but a radical solution offered any hope.

6. His was a final revolt against always being a member of the weaker minority group. It was an assertion of self, of independence, of Herzl's native pride. It was the final negation of all apologetics, and the recognition that a solution for the whole people must be sought.

7. Notice how the new vision of Zionism (not yet called that) at once galvanized his whole personality into action. The playwright and journalist became a man of action, political action.

8. Why were the rich assimilated Jews opposed to him? Why in terms of Lewin?

9. What great qualities made Herzl able to crystalize a world movement where before there had been only sporadic groups and unharnessed longings?

10. Explain how the Jewish tragedy became the driving force behind Herzl's plan.

11. What was his diagnosis of the Jewish position in Central Europe? Have facts justified his pessimism?

12. Why did Herzl think that the Jewish question must be presented as a political world question?

13. Why did he insist on "public recognition?" He sensed the danger inherent in slow infiltration into Palestine of small colonies unprotected by political recognition, as there of right and not on sufferance. Have not the last twenty years under the Balfour Declaration justified his demand for national action and world recognition of the Jewish settlement in Palestine?

14. Notice that only after he realizes that "we are a people" does he develop a plan that gives him both satisfaction and direction.

COLLATERAL READING

1. Read some of Herzl's own writings: *Excerpts from Herzl's Diaries*, and *The Jewish State*, both published by Scopus Publishing Co., New York.

2. Excellent material on every facet of Herzl's life is to be found in the *Herzl Memorial* volume published in 1929, by The New Palestine (Many synagogues and schools have copies of this book.)

3. There is also a brilliant pamphlet by Emanuel Neumann: *The Birth of Jewish Statesmanship*, a story of Theodore Herzl's life.

CONCLUSION

In the introduction, we said that this study unit "is designed to help you make the important decision about what your relation to the Jewish people will be." Can you judge the issues more clearly now that you have become intimately acquainted with the varied experiences and the profound searching of soul of these men and women?

This at least, Kurt Lewin makes clear. As long as you know nothing of Israel and see it only as a small people, hounded from land to land, always an unwelcome minority, so long is there the danger that you too may contract the disease of self-hatred, in one form or another. But when you can experience its rich resources from within, the Jewish people will no longer seem mean or pitiful to you. Then the realization that the Bible was written in Hebrew by Jews, and that this book has become the Bible of half of mankind; that Jews found an outlook on life for themselves so inspiring that it has become the basis for western civilization as well, will give you a consciousness of being well born—in being born a Jew.

Dr. Steinberger never learned much about his people, except for a few generalities in the book, *The Discourses of Keidansky*. He struggled and continues to struggle, therefore, against being classified as a Jew. To him, being a Jew never meant more than an irritating handicap. Naturally, he was unwilling to accept the Jewish people or to acknowledge that their destiny is his. He remains to this day, a man caught in a snare from which he can never escape, but unable ever to forget his anomalous position.

Dr. Steinberger's dilemma illustrates, too, the main thesis of Namier. No individual solution is possible for a Jew; the world reacts to the Jewish *people* as a community. No polish, no degree of assimilation can change the fact that Dr. Steinberger is still a Jew in the eyes of the world. If and when the Jewish people as a whole finds peace and achieves status, *your* position will be of a more normal and happy one. Namier stresses the interdependence between the individual and his people; Lewin focuses on the individual. The two points of view supplement each other.

Marian Sanders and Jessie Sampter are both well-to-do, cultured American Jews, not very different in background from Dr. Steinberger. But more fortunate, for both found their people before it was too late! Marian was sufficiently aware of being a Jew by birth to be made uncomfortable by the fact and was more than a little ashamed of it; she was unable to acquire that sureness and balance to which her status in society and her own gifts entitled her. By accident she met the people of Israel, suddenly, face to face as it were—in Eretz Yisrael. And at once she understood, intuitively, where she belonged, where and how she could best develop. She threw in her lot with her people, learned their language (Hebrew) and its literature. She saw Israel, real and earthy in the Land, met Jews there who lived freely, without ever a thought "to the Gentile looking over their shoulders." And she, too, was refreshed and at last set free.

No two human beings ever have exactly the same experiences. Jessie Sampter, the sensitive poet, found and lost herself, as it were, several times before she, too, recognized the basic fact of the Jewish people; it was but another short step to Zionism. Then there is a sudden release of energy. The Jew in Palestine is proud and free to create and Jessie Sampter shares in this gift by her conscious identification with Israel.

In Herzl there is little of this search for personal Jewish orientation. As an adolescent and young adult "the Jewish world, whose inferior position always wounded his pride . . . drifted further and further out of his mind." He became a successful playwright and a brilliant journalist. He knew he was a Jew and he knew there was anti-Semitism but these facts remained on the periphery of his mind. Consciously, he was part of the great liberal intellectual life of Europe in the 1880's. Here and there he ventured on some scheme for the solution of the Jewish problem, but on the whole, he was only rarely concerned with Jewry.

And then suddenly, the full force of the Frenchman's hatred of Dreyfus, the Jew, hit Herzl like a whiplash. At once he realized that no palliatory measures could ever permanently mend the situation of the Jews; that no individual Jew could ever count on being exempted from this hatred, and that liberalism was no insurance against anti-Semitism. He is aflame with his discovery that the only remedy lies in political action for and by the Jewish *people*. He is galvanized into action; he completely identifies himself with his people. Herzl feels it is possible to change "the inferior Jewish position"—by migration into the Promised Land. Now he is able to say: "We are a people . . . The folk personality of the Jewish people cannot, must not and does not want to go under . . . . The world will be liberated by our liberation . . . . made greater by our greatness. And that which we seek here for our own use will stream out mightily and beneficiently upon all mankind."

In many ways Brandeis is not unlike Herzl. He had had very little Jewish training in his youth; he had attained an important position in American life; he had apparently not himself suffered from anti-Semitism. Unlike Herzl he was not even brought face to face with a public demonstration of Jew-hatred. But when the need of the Jewish people was presented to him, by De Haas and others, Brandeis at once felt it as his own. His Jewish studies, undertaken at this time, convinced him that the Jews *are* a people. As an American, Brandeis believed firmly in the right of every individual—and of every people—to life, liberty and the pursuit of happiness. But he carried the implications of this tenet further. He declared it not only the right but the *duty* of every people to seek freedom and happiness. Thus Brandeis made a peculiarly American contribution to Zionist thought—there is laid upon the Jewish people the duty to struggle for its freedom, through Zionism; not only can no Jew be truly free and happy until Israel is free, but "to be good Americans we must be better Jews, and to be better Jews we must become Zionists."

Once you make your decision and you accept Zionism, you have laid upon you three basic duties:

1. *To the People of Israel:* To take an active part in every aspect of Jewish life. "Do not separate yourself from the community."

2. *To the Land of Israel:* To feel that upon your shoulders, too, rests upon the responsibiilty for the "Binyan Haaretz" (the rebuilding of the Land). In the words of Brandeis: "We need

many, many men—soldiers in the cause of liberty who will give of their effort and resources in unfailing and ever strengthening support" to the new Zion.

3. *To the Cultural Inheritance of Israel:* To have a reverential attitude towards Jewish tradition and culture, towards its language (Hebrew) and its literature, towards its ideas and ideals. To study, to acquire as much as you can of Jewish knowledge and culture.

If to be a Zionist implies all these attitudes and actions, then to accept Zionism is to take a conscious, decisive step as a Jew; it is to stand firm and happy before all the world with confidence in the Jew and *as* a Jew.